What Color is

the Sky

The world of investing is full of illusions that

stop you from seeing reality. If you push the

clouds aside, the truth will appear.

DISCLAIMER

This book contains the opinions and ideas of its author. It is sold with the understanding that neither the author nor the publisher are engaged in rendering investment, financial, accounting, legal, tax, insurance, or other professional advice or services. If you require such advice or services, a competent professional should be consulted. The strategies outlined in may not be suitable for every person and are not guaranteed to produce any particular result.

No warrant is made with respect to the accuracy or completeness of the information contained herein. Both the author and publisher specifically disclaim any responsibility for any liability, loss, or risk, personal and otherwise, which is incurred as a consequence, directly or indirectly, of the use and application of any of the contents of this book.

Here is the same speech put in a way you can actually understand. I am trying to educate you, not "sell" you. No one is paying me to hype his or her products. This book is designed to educate you so you can make good decisions with your money and avoid the bad one's.

No individual situation is the same. One way does not work for everyone. I realize many people struggle to just survive in this world. You may find yourself in a situation where you have few options. I encourage you to find ways to apply what you read in this book as best you can. Education can help when life seems hopeless.

Find ways around the obstacles in your life. The power lies within you and your ability to change the way you think and act. Never forget that, and never give up. You truly do have the ability to change the course of your life. Believe that, and believe in yourself.

This book is dedicated to John Bogle.

Mr. Bogle has done more to help the individual investor, and the institutional investor indirectly, than any person who has come before or after him. I hope to share his wisdom throughout the following pages. It could not have happened without the work he has done. Thank you, John Bogle, for standing up for what was right when others would not. You are a true hero in the eyes of many.

CONTENTS

Stage II: **INVESTORS BEWARE!**

Stage III: **THE PATH FORWARD**

Stage IV: **PUTTING THE PIECES TOGETHER**

Stage V: **FINAL THOUGHTS**

What Color is the Sky?

My name is Mike Finley, and I am known as The Crazy Man in the Pink Wig. I wrote the book, *Financial Happine$$,* and I built the website, thecrazymaninthepinkwig.com, to help people develop a better relationship with their money. I have identified a path toward taking control of one's life as a person takes control of their money. This book deals with the world of investing and the many pitfalls that you must avoid.

What Color is the Sky is my way of showing you that what you see may simply be an illusion. That illusion could cost you a great deal of money, stress, and time. Once upon a time…

A young boy was gazing into the big beautiful blue sky as he enjoyed a perfect summer day. Up walked an old man who greeted the young lad with a warm smile. The old man took a good hard look at the sky and then gazed over at the young boy before asking a simple question:

What color is the sky?

The young boy looked at the old man and said, "It's blue, old man. Can't you see?" The old man looked at the young boy and said, "It's black." The young boy turned to look at the sky again. It was blue! He then looked at the old man and said, "Are you blind, old man. It's blue!" The old man smiled and stated once again with plenty of confidence, "It's black, young fella," as he walked away. What color was the sky?

The young boy decided that he had three options.

- **Option 1:** Write off the old man as crazy and ignore his ramblings.

- **Option 2:** Believe the old man because he is old and wise.

- **Option 3:** Research the subject.

The young boy selected option 3. He started talking to his friends and family and they all said the sky was blue, but were they experts on the sky? The young lad decided to seek out the true experts and that led him to people who study the stars and the vast universe beyond the Earth. He identified astronomers who knew the truth.

What did he find? The sky is actually black! The reason it looks blue in the daytime is because of those light particles from the sun as the air scatters blue sunlight more than it does red. His eyes had played tricks on him. What he thought he saw was merely an illusion. He perceived a blue sky, but that was not the actual color. The old man was right. It's black!

Let's fast forward. Over time, the young boy became the old man as all young boys do. The now, old man, found himself walking outside and gazing into a beautiful blue sky on a lovely spring day and what did he see: a young boy looking up into the sky. The old man walked up to the young lad and greeted him with a question that was posed to him many years ago:

What color is the sky?

There is a message that will resonate throughout this manuscript. What you "see" when looking at Wall Street and your investment options may be nothing more than an illusion. You perceive one thing, but reality is something totally different. This may be hard for you to accept. It was for me, but I did my research and I have the answers that you need if you want to become the wise and successful investor.

I ask you to open your mind to the possibility that what you know could be wrong and what you don't know could change the course of your life. Not so sure? Good. Stay skeptical, but don't just brush me off as some old man who has "lost it." The future belongs to those who challenge the world around them. Make that you!

"The first step toward change is awareness. The second step is acceptance."

- **Nathaniel Branden**

Foreword

We met Mike Finley by phone. That first phone call was less a conversation than an interrogation! He had found us through NAPFA, a Fee-Only organization's website, and he had called to check out whether we were legitimate. Mike's criteria were that we were true Fee-Only fiduciaries (did not sell any financial products of any kind, ever, and put our clients' interests ahead of our own), and that we were proponents of index investing, as he is. We are Fee-Only, commission-free financial advisors and fiduciaries who use passive investments, and Mike verified in-depth that we actually believe in and practice what our website says we do.

Our answers satisfied Mike to the extent that he asked to meet; but in truth, we were as suspicious of him as he was of us. Who was The "Crazy" Man in the Pink Wig? He claimed to be offering free education to college students, professors, and townspeople at the University of Northern Iowa. Were we actually to believe that he received no personal gain of any kind through these "free" classes?

Could this guy truly be so driven to teaching others the knowledge he had gained from years of studying personal finance and investing that he would volunteer his time to teach these courses? It seemed unlikely, but we did agree to that first meeting. What developed is a friendship and professional regard between people with passionately held beliefs.

Mike Finley is exactly who and what he claims to be, and he works harder at giving away his time and knowledge than most people would devote to a full-time, high-paying job.

This book walks the personal investor through the terminology, the process and the explanations necessary for sound, long-term investing, (the who, what, how and why of personal finance). He does a better job of speaking to an uncertain or inexperienced investor than other books on the market, because Mike himself has walked this path. He is perhaps the most well read colleague we have. He never has enough knowledge.

Mike knows what he wants his students to learn, and he tells them what they need to know with a no-nonsense, straightforward delivery. His style is direct, informative, and compelling.

Mike has the conviction, which we wholeheartedly share, that a person can change his or her life by taking responsibility for and control of his/her finances. He tells you like it is. Most of the financial service providers are primarily selling products.

What Color is the Sky guides readers on a path to successful lifetime investing. Mike's writing style breaks down investment terms and techniques to their fundamental parts. He explains the pros and cons of each of the investment techniques. The book builds logically to teach you, the reader, to develop your own well allocated, well diversified, low cost, easy to manage portfolio.

Mike provides you with the tools to begin with a basic portfolio. He also explains how to increase the portfolio's complexity and the management required to maintain it if you wish to do so. You decide the level you are comfortable handling –whether to keep a basic, easy to manage portfolio or to challenge yourself with more difficult and time-consuming configurations. The beauty is that there is no right or wrong approach; you get to choose what fits best with your particular situation.

Absorb its wisdom and believe that you have the capacity to apply its concepts to your own finances. Whether you ultimately decide to manage your own portfolio or to delegate that job to others, your knowledge will prevent anyone from taking advantage of you. Confidence in the management of your investments can bring a welcome sense of comfort and peace to your financial future and other aspects of your life.

Sincerely,
Jean and Eric Mote
Mote Wealth Management, LLC
CERTIFIED FINANCIAL PLANNER™ Practitioners
NAPFA-Registered Financial Advisors

Testimonials

"I have been introduced to a new world filled with information which neither my Finance Degree nor the people I'm surrounded by could've ever educated me on personal finance. I am able to pursue my financial happiness based on the resources Michael has suggested and by taking action to further my own education." —**Leora**, Student, Age 20

"As a Nepali student, I was never taught about money or anything to do with personal finance. Mike is an outstanding teacher regarding this issue because his teachings are not just about managing money but also about living a happier and a better life." —**Parimal,** Student, Age 21

"…I have gone from depleted bank accounts to riches by Mike's teaching in a very short time. He continues to change my now and future world of life and money daily. It is without question that Mike will change YOUR life too." —**Daniel**, U.S. Army Military Officer, Age 22

"…After the first class of Mike's, I was hooked. I studied. I read. I wanted to know it all. I wanted to get my financial life straight. I can finally say that I'm a confident woman when it comes to my personal finances. I want to encourage every woman to become financially literate and to study and read on her own. Don't just leave it to the man." —**Jenna**, Real Estate Portfolio Analyst, Age 24

"Mike's well-researched investment advice gives me complete confidence in my investment decisions. The power of his strategy lies in how simple it is to apply immediately." —**Trevor**, Actuary, Age 24

"The truth heard one time can sound stranger than a lie heard 1000 times. What Mike says might initially sound strange because it's not how society talks about money. I thought I was on a good path with investing but learned that trying to pick stocks and investing in random funds is risky. Now I am on a clear path. Money is a tool and Mike is showing you how to use the tool to reach your goals." —**Axel**, Mechanical Engineer, Age 25

"Mike has motivated me to take control of my life. He has opened my eyes to the power of being financially free and doing what I want in life, simply by educating myself and investing in no load index mutual funds ..." — **Casey**, High School Teacher/Activities Director, Age 26

"The financial service industry is a marketing machine out to convince the average consumer that bloated expensive products are best. Mike is arming the consumer with their best weapon—financial literacy." —**Tracy**, Former Financial Advisor and Insurance Agent, Age 32

"Many of us remember a special teacher who took a complicated (or boring) subject and presented it in an inspiring way. Mike Finley is that kind of teacher. The information that he shares about investing has given me greater confidence in my ability..." —**Jean**, Ministry Support, Age 48

"For years, advisors avoided guiding me down the best investment-path... Their guidance was to benefit their revenue stream. Mike has completely opened my eyes to the strategy lurking within the industry." —**Heidi**, mom/business woman, Age unknown (just teasing...48)

"The confidence I have gained from Mike's motivational classes and his belief in me has allowed me to take control of my investments and my journey towards financial freedom." —**Lisa**, Educator, Age 49

"Saving, investing and living below your means takes discipline. Mike has taught me how to invest and manage money going into my retirement years..." —**Rick**, Retired FedEx Courier, Age 60

"...How could I take the time to learn everything I thought I needed to learn to be able to invest safely and smartly? I just didn't have time. Mike made it simple through his sage advice and resources, showing me that not only did I have the time; but also through a few simple steps, I could take control of my financial future." —**Cynthia**, Professor, Age 61

"Thanks to Mike, I have gone from knowing nothing about investing and letting someone else do it for me, to managing my investments on my own with comfort and confidence..." —**Anne**, Retired, Age 74

Introduction

Get ready! I intend to take you on a journey of self-discovery, which will ultimately provide you the education you will need to become a wise and successful investor. The world of investing is understood by a select few. You can be one of them. It does not require a high IQ nor does it demand years and years of study on the issue.

What does it require? (1) Your eagerness to learn. (2) Your belief in yourself. (3) Your willingness to challenge conventional wisdom. (4) Your ability to identify the wrong sources when receiving investment advice. (5) Your skill in identifying the right sources that will lead you down the right path. (6) Your motivation to act on what you learn. (7) Your stubbornness to stay the course when times get difficult.

That is a rather challenging list, don't you think? You might even call it daunting. Notice how each point starts with YOUR? It's up to you. I will help you, and I will guide you toward others who will help you. Ultimately though, it will be up to you. YOU are the answer!

Here is the disclaimer. I cannot promise you guaranteed returns. I cannot promise you wealth. Actually, I can promise you very little. What I will do is provide you an education that you can use to change the way you invest your money. What you do with that education will eventually provide you the answers to what your future may look like. Life is a roller coaster and so is this book. Hang on!

You need to know not only what to do, but also what not to do. Here is a little secret that you will hear time and again throughout this book. The financial industry and its "helpers," rake in billions of dollars every year because the average person doesn't have a clue about investing and the industry that "helps" you. Don't be one of those people! Start learning from the right sources as you move away from the wrong sources. *What Color is the Sky* will help you do just that.

What you will learn comes from peer-reviewed research (data can be found in gray throughout the book). Translated: You learn the truth and then apply it in real life to your own individual portfolios as you grow your accounts over time. You can learn more at thecrazymaninthepinkwig.com.

Now is the time to identify your team. The list of individuals below will guide you as they have guided me. These are the true experts, not the charlatans and the crooks that you see far too often.

- Paul Samuelson
- Merton Miller
- William Sharpe
- Daniel Kahneman
- Eugene Fama
- John Bogle
- Charles Ellis
- Burton Malkiel
- David Swensen
- Jack Meyer
- William Bernstein
- Daniel Solin
- Frank Armstrong III
- Larry Swedroe
- Rick Ferri

That team includes five Nobel Laureates in Economics and some of the most respected and knowledgeable men in the financial industry. There is one more guy on my team. His name is Warren Buffett. Let's go!

"There is no end to education. It is not that you read a book, pass an examination, and finish with education. The whole of life, from the moment you are born to the moment you die, is a process of learning."

- **Jiddu Krishnamurti**

Stage I

THE JOURNEY

1

BEFORE YOU START

It is very important to "get your house in order" prior to investing your money. This means dealing with your debt responsibly, protecting yourself with insurance, and putting some money aside for emergencies that you can tap immediately if needed.

First, let's tackle the debt issue. If you are paying double-digit interest rates on debt, put your extra money toward that debt. It's a no-brainer. If you are paying 20% on your credit card and you make extra payments to that card, you are earning a guaranteed 20%. No investment will beat that over time. Pay off the credit card!

What if your interest rates on debt are below 10%? It depends. Here is what I would do. If I had debt with interest rates above 6%, I would pay extra toward the debt before investing. (There is an exception. I would always invest in my company retirement plan up to the matching amount of FREE money.)

If I had debt with interest rates below 6%, I would take extra money and put it toward the retirement plan at work and/or a Roth IRA and simply make the required payments on my debt, but no more. You might even do a bit of both if that strikes you as a balanced approach.

Ultimately, it is your call on how you deal with the debt in your life. The key is to identify a specific number that you will use that will help you decide whether to pay down debt or invest your money or both. Whether you choose 6% or some other number, just be sure to give it some real thought prior to making the decision. This will be a BIG decision that will have a big impact on your future. Think it through carefully.

Next, how do you approach the emergency fund? I break this down in two ways. You can go super safe and keep the money in the bank/credit union or you can put it in a money market fund or bond fund at a place like Vanguard (more on Vanguard later in the book). **BIG POINT:** I am not compensated in any way by Vanguard. They do this investing thing better than most. That's why I recommend them. Thank John Bogle for that.

Option 1 could be the bank/credit union. This provides you protection from market risk (the ups and downs of stock and bond markets for example), but it does nothing regarding inflation risk. There is NO risk-free investment. If you go this route, try to find ways to increase your interest on the money. Online banks may be one option.

Option 2 (my preferred option) would involve a money market fund or bond fund at vanguard.com. You are taking slightly more risk and in turn, you should see slightly higher returns. Basically, you are trying to stay up with inflation. I recommend money market funds when they are paying 3% and bond funds when they aren't (currently the case in 2015).

What funds? At Vanguard, I recommend the Money Market Prime and regarding the bond funds, I recommend the Total Bond Market Index Fund (more risk with rising interest rates) or the Short-Term Bond Index Fund (less risk with rising interest rates). How much? I would stick with the usual recommendation of three to six months of living expenses. Next up, the world of investing!

"Saving is a bargain compared to spending. Every dollar we earn and then spend will be subject to federal, state, payroll, and sales taxes, so maybe we end up with 60 or 70 cents' worth of merchandise. Meanwhile, if we stash that dollar in our employer's 401(k) plan, we get to keep the entire dollar and we can leave it to grow tax-deferred. We may even get a matching company contribution, so our dollar immediately turns into $1.50 or $2."

- **Jonathon Clements,** *The Little Book of Main Street Money*

2

THE FINANCIAL LITERACY
JOURNEY

This chapter was taken out of *Financial Happine$$*. I recommend you apply it to your life going forward. It will serve you well as you continue down your path toward success as an investor.

- **I am.** I am the answer to my financial future. I can make it a total mess, or I can make it a glorious masterpiece. All of this hinges on me. I am the answer.

- **Knowledge.** I must educate myself before making financial decisions. This will involve a commitment to education outside the classroom with teachers, not salespeople.

- **ACTION.** I must take action with what I learn. Being financially smart and doing nothing with the information will accomplish nothing. I must get it done!

- **Keep Doing.** I must keep doing what is right financially one week, one month, one year, and one decade at a time. I will stay persistent as I develop the right habits (pay myself first automatically at the beginning of the month) that I perform time and time again.

- **Just say NO!** I will say no to materialism (defining myself by the stuff I own) and the crocodiles (salespeople who feed off my financial ignorance). This will free up money to be saved, invested, and given away.

- **Patience.** Time is on my side. Be patient as my financial plan unfolds over long periods of time. Get rich slowly through compound interest. My money will make me money.

- **Financial Freedom.** Financial freedom can be achieved if I am willing to truly commit myself totally to the process of following through on my financial plan. Saving = Freedom = Opportunities.

- **Live MY Dreams.** Live the life of my dreams and not someone else's. Financial freedom provides me the opportunity to do just that. Find my path, and live it!

- **Give.** Live to give. Learning to be grateful for what I have and identify ways to give unconditionally, will set me free. Giving to the people and organizations I believe in will bring meaning and inner peace to my life.

- **Happiness.** Happiness comes to those who follow their dreams and share what they know and have with others. I want to be happy. I will be happy. The answers to life are found in me.

The opportunities to change the course of your life and achieve the ultimate prize of true happiness are there when you are ready to act on what you learn here and with the books I will reference all along the way. Join me in this journey. It will change the course of your life.

"When I was 5 years old, my mother always told me that happiness was the key to life. When I went to school, they asked me what I wanted to be when I grew up. I wrote down "happy." They told me I didn't understand the assignment, and I told them they didn't understand life."

- **Anonymous**

3

THE BLANK SLATE

When you start down the road toward becoming a better investor you should first ask yourself, "What do I know, and who did I learn it from?" I want to ask a favor of you. I want you to take an eraser and clear off that slate in your head that contains your investment knowledge. I want you to start with a blank slate.

Why a blank slate? What many people know has been placed in their memory bank by the financial industry and its "helpers" who have a conflict of interest with the information they share with you. Translated? They educate you in ways that bring you to them and their expensive products and services that make THEM a lot of money.

Did that sound a bit harsh? I hope so. It was meant to wake you up to the reality of the situation. The financial services industry has built a business model that works very well for them, not you. The faster you learn this key point, the quicker you can move on to better options that have been made available to you.

Let's go back in time a bit. I was 20 years old when I started learning about investing. Who was teaching me? Two very nice, well dressed, properly registered "helpers." One was a fee-based financial advisor and the other was a life insurance agent who really liked whole life insurance. They "sold" me on expensive products that earned them big fat loads and commissions. My ignorance cost me dearly.

When a person with experience meets a person with money, the person with experience gets the money and the person with the money gets the experience. I screwed up. Shame on me.

I lived with that education for five long years. Why? I saw these men as the true experts. They had age, experience, credentials, suits, and financial knowledge. Here is the truth that I learned years later. They were salespeople! They are not the true experts and they never were. They are given products to sell and they peddle them as best they can. They also spend a great deal of time selling themselves. I fell for it!

Why do I share this story with you? We have all made mistakes along the way. We trusted when maybe we shouldn't. We jumped in when maybe we should have paused. Life is a bit of a crapshoot, and sometimes we end up screwing up even when we are trying to do the right thing.

Let go of the past. We can start over. That is the past and this is the present as you prepare for your future. I admit my mistakes. I recommend you do the same. Wipe that slate clean and start anew. It worked for me and it can work for you.

Now is when you start educating yourself from independent sources that don't sell products and services. Get rid of the conflicts of interest. That will push you away from many of the high cost investments that you don't need and into some very inexpensive investments that you do need. This requires a new way of thinking.

You can do this. As you proceed forward, keep reminding yourself that you are quite capable of learning and applying that knowledge to your life. I will continue to walk you down the path toward becoming the wise and successful investor as you avoid the financial industry and its many "helpers." Onward!

"A smart man makes a mistake, learns from it, and never makes that mistake again. But a wise man finds a smart man and learns from him how to avoid the mistake altogether."
                                                    - **Roy H. Williams**

4

THE ENEMY

I know who your biggest enemy is. How could I know? I have an understanding of human nature and what lies beneath the surface. Your biggest enemy is no different than my biggest enemy. Your biggest enemy (and your best friend with the proper education) is that person staring back at you from the mirror.

The sooner in life you learn this truth, the faster you can proceed toward the life that is waiting for you. Understanding this mystifying world of investing can help you in some very positive ways, but first, you must take the time to recognize who is holding you back.

Now, I know many of you out there might be shaking your head or possibly just be confused by this message. That's okay. I would have been confused as well many years ago. That is until I accepted the reality of the situation as my education increased. I recognized the fact that I was my own worst enemy. Here is where it gets kind of cool.

It is not a bad thing to understand that you are the biggest enemy in your life. Actually, it's empowering. Why? Because you can change! There are many things in life that are beyond your control. And when I say many, I mean most. What is within your control is YOU.

You can change. You can change your mindset. You can change your attitude. You can change the way you think. You can even change the way you behave. You can become a new person. Stop and read that last sentence again, please. YOU have the ability to change the course of your life, as you become a successful investor.

Am I overstating the case? No. Actually, I am probably understating the situation. The ability of the individual to overcome the difficulties of life and come out the other side with a new perspective is a very powerful weapon. It's a transformation.

You allow your old self to die (metaphorically), so your new self can be created. You can take what you have learned from the past and create your new life. You become the new YOU.

Do you think I am a little "out there" with this kind of thinking? It's okay. I am crazy and I don't apologize for that. I am crazy enough to think I can change my life when I am ready to embrace that part of me that is waiting to be released. I am crazy enough to act on what I learn to make that better life a reality. I embrace a new way of thinking and I encourage you to do the same. Being "crazy" can be very liberating.

Are you open to a new way of thinking? I don't need an answer at this very moment. I simply want you to open your mind to the possibilities of what your life could be with a new way of thinking. I would like you to demonstrate to all, including yourself that you have left your old self behind as you embrace this new version of who you will become.

Change starts in your mind and then it gradually builds as you develop the habits that drive the behaviors that will cause you to go in a different direction with your life. You can be reborn into the new you as you create your new life. Awake to the possibilities of YOU.

"Try to keep your soul young and quivering right up to old age, and to imagine right up to the brink of death that life is only beginning. I think that is the only way to keep adding to one's talent, to one's affections, and to one's inner happiness."
- **George Sand**

5

THE DEFAULT SETTING

The default setting is fixed at birth. It makes up about 50% of who you are and there is little you can do about it. What is the default setting? Here I am talking about your genetics.

The genes you were born with play a big part in who you are today. There is virtually nothing you can do about that 50% you received from the people who brought you into this world, but that leaves 50% that can be changed and that is something worth thinking about.

The other 50% of who you are and who you're going to be will be up to you based on the environments you find yourself in, the people you spend time with, and how you react throughout that time. You get to have a major impact on that 50%.

There is quite a bit of research on this subject. We know that genetics tells us a lot about who you are. Your default setting not only tells us about how you look, but also how you think and feel. That is a big deal and I am not about to discount it, but there is more to the story as they say.

Are you a "glass half empty" kind of person or a "glass half full" kind of person? Have you given this much thought? Can you provide an answer that is not biased? It's pretty hard for some people. We don't always see ourselves as others see us.

Here is an easy way to answer that question without too much effort by you. Ask the people around you. They know you and they will be able to answer this question of ½ full or ½ empty relatively quickly if they are willing to be honest with you on the subject.

Why is it important to identify your default setting? You want to identify how you filter information when it comes into your life. Looking within will help you understand how you came to this moment in time.

Do you see the negative or the positive first when information is provided to you? Is your first thought to criticize others or to praise them? I am not asking you to judge yourself, just identify who you are based on your genetic code. Now let's look at what can be modified.

Are you open to learning new and different ideas and concepts? My guess is you probably are or you wouldn't be reading this book. You are probably open to learning. Just keep in mind, many people would never pick up a book like this and read it from start to finish. You are unique!

Once you become open-minded to the possibility of change on a fundamental level, you will change. Take a moment and think about that last sentence. The research tells us that you have the ability to change half of who you are throughout your lifetime. That is huge!

Why would you want to change so much? Because there is so much to learn, that's why! We are all capable of changing in some very big ways. Why not become more? Why not you?

Even if your default setting is negative, you can change. Keep reminding yourself that you can change 50% of who you are. Believe in that and believe in YOU.

"People are always blaming their circumstances for what they are. I don't believe in circumstances. The people who get on in this world are the people who get up and look for the circumstances they want, and, if they can't find them, make them."

- **George Bernard Shaw**

6

CHANGE IS NOT EASY

There will always be people who resist change. Change is tough. Change is scary. It's important to accept this reality as you set out on this journey I speak of. It is critically important that you are open to changing the way you think and behave. Growth follows change. Keep reminding yourself about that key point.

We can only help others when they are ready to be helped. We can push, we can nudge, we can even beg people to change, but ultimately, it will be up to them. I ask you to not resist the discomfort that some of this information will cause you. That simply means growth is happening. This book was written for the beginner, intermediate and advanced investor. Little by little, we all have the ability to advance as we change and grow.

So what does it take for someone to "be ready" for change? That's a tough question. Here is what I have learned: Human beings learn incrementally over time. They connect the dots one concept after another based on what they are exposed to.

You can only connect dots that you can see, and in many cases feel. Feel? Change occurs not so much when you reach a person's brain, but when you reach their heart and quite possibly, their soul. That is when many people start to transform the way they think, behave and live.

How does a person reach others? You demonstrate through your life. You set the example that you are trying to share with others. You help others by helping yourself. Basically, you fix YOU. That is the one thing you have full control over. Others will see that and consider the thought of changing themselves. Set that example.

People transform first in their heart and soul, then in their brain, and finally in their actions. This is what I have learned and experienced over my lifetime. Change takes time. Do not expect immediate results simply because you change something today.

Here is a big point that should help. The decisions and actions you make today will provide insight into what your future will look like many years down the road.

The future will be shaped by what you do today.

Making well informed financial decisions today may or may not change your current situation at this moment in time. It is important to be patient with the process.

This is a journey that will involve obstacles and difficulties. I am not promising smooth sailing, but I do promise you an interesting trip. Stay with me as I show you worlds that you may have never seen before.

You have to take that leap of faith in believing that the information you will learn in this book will payoff as time goes on. It is time to reshape your future.

The information I share with you as well as the books I reference are designed to help you with your future, which could be the next 10 years, the next 30 years, or maybe the next 50 years! We are preparing for a voyage that can change the course of your life. Let's go!

"You must be the change you wish to see in the world."

- **Mahatma Gandhi**

7

YOU CAN DO IT

You can do it? Do what? You can be your own investment advisor as you take control of your future. You are quite capably of becoming a great investor. How do I define a great investor? Based on the time period, your returns after costs and taxes are higher than the vast majority of investors in the world. You can do that. You can outperform all kinds of people with all kinds of backgrounds and all kinds of IQs.

Now some of you might be thinking that I am setting the bar rather high. I don't think so. You see, I know you can do it, if you are willing to take the time to believe in yourself, educate yourself on the world of investing, and finally, apply what you learn to your current situation. How do I know you can do it? I did it and I have seen many others do it.

I just planted a seed that I hope will grow over time. It's going to be up to you to nourish that seed and help it become something pretty amazing one day. Here is something to keep in mind: *Do what is difficult and life will be easy. Do what is easy and life will be difficult.*

Long ago, the first "money book" I read planted that seed in my head. I took a chance and believed in myself. It wasn't easy. It was a bit scary actually. I had no clue about how to invest my money and yet, I took that leap of faith in believing I could learn. Now it's your turn.

There is plenty to learn on this subject. I hope to provide you with the answers you will need, as you become an informed, wise, and successful investor for a very long time. But, I need you to believe in YOU. It really is that simple. The rest is nothing more than a slow steady accumulation of knowledge followed by action.

You do not need a finance degree, a business degree, or any degree at all to become a successful investor. What do you need? I need you to believe in YOU and be open to new information. It is very important that you choose to become that person. Yes, I said CHOOSE. I'm the guy who tells you that the world you live in is the world you have created for yourself. If you want a new life, create it!

Becoming a great investor will require specific habits and behaviors. Those habits and behaviors will in many cases, spill over into other parts of your life and provide positive improvements where you didn't actually attempt to change. These are called "keystone habits." Read the book, *The Power of Habit*, by Charles Duhigg for a more detailed explanation.

Here is one habit I need you to acquire right now. Start saving your money consistently and automatically over time. Select a set amount of money and save it into your company retirement plan, Roth IRA and/or outside of tax-sheltered accounts immediately upon getting paid (you could also use that savings to pay down debt). Becoming a great investor is a wonderful goal, but you must develop the skillset of a great saver to make it life changing.

How much should you save? Save at least 10% of your gross income (before taxes are withheld). Work at getting that number up to 20% as time goes on. This will provide you the capital that you need to invest in markets all over the world. This is a very big deal! You must focus on becoming a great saver as you develop into becoming a great investor.

Becoming a great saver and a great investor can and will create a new life for you and the people around you. I need you to believe me when I say that. It worked for me and it can work for you. This is your time!

"Always be a first-rate version of yourself, instead of a second-rate version of somebody else."
   - Judy Garland

8

THE BRAIN

I am going to push you in many different directions as this book unfolds. I will be asking your brain to work overtime. That's where change originates, as you become exposed to new information that moves you in new directions.

This could get puzzling at times, and it is quite possible that I will challenge what you are currently doing right now when it comes to handling money and investing it (if you are). I need you to keep that brain open to new information.

The human brain is an amazing organ. It processes information at incredible speeds and holds data from your past that you thought was lost forever. **Some of that data is wrong!**

Some of what goes on in your brain is not helping you and has hurt you in the past. How do I know this? You're human, just like me. Your brain is not always leading you in the right direction. This chapter deals with some of the negative messages that you are receiving on a daily basis.

We use the brain to receive and process what we experience. We also use it to formulate patterns in everyday life, even when there are no patterns. The brain takes all of that information and attempts to see the projected future. It also helps you identify what is known. It's not always right. As a matter of fact, it can be dead wrong!

Let's take a look at a few messages that your brain may be sending you, and you can decide for yourself if any of these messages are a little bit wrong, or maybe a lot wrong.

- I am not smart enough to invest.
- I need a finance or business degree to be a good investor.
- I don't make enough money to invest.
- Investing is gambling.
- Investing in the stock market is rigged and I can't win.
- Investing is for rich people, not me.
- I have to be a numbers person to invest.
- It's too difficult to invest.
- It's too expensive to invest.
- I'm too young.
- I'm too old.
- The future isn't worth investing in.

That's a pretty big list! Do any of them pertain to you? Here are the facts. All of those statements are wrong. It's important to understand the incorrect information when it pops up in your head.

The brain makes mistakes. All that processing doesn't always shoot out the right answer. I'm sure some of you have heard, *garbage in, garbage out*. Sometimes the brain shoots out the wrong answer when it's given the wrong information. It's important to know that.

I want you to take that negative information that you currently have floating around in your brain and replace it with the information you learn in the following pages. It's time to take out the garbage.

"You will never be free until you free yourself from the prison of your own false thoughts."

- Philip Arnold

9

THE FLAPPER

Do you know what a flapper is? Not to worry if you don't, I will share all I know on the matter and I will also attempt to demonstrate what a flapper and becoming the wise and successful investor have in common. Prepare yourself; we will be entering the bathroom and ultimately into the world of toilets!

A flapper is that rubber device that resides in your toilet tank. It is the moving part of the flush valve that lets water pass and stops it when the tank needs to fill. It appears pretty harmless, but problems arise when it fails. You see, the flapper with the little chain and rubber attachment tends to deteriorate over time like all parts do and that requires the homeowner to replace it on occasion.

The first time I had to fix one of these things, it was not pretty. (I am better at breaking things than fixing them.) I could have called a plumber who would have taken care of this simple procedure quickly, but I was willing to try my hand at what appeared to be a simple fix. It took me more than an hour to get the job done. When I finished, I needed therapy and a good stiff drink!

A few years later, I had to fix the darn thing again. It took me about 30 minutes that time. Now let's fast-forward about two decades. I just replaced the flapper for the 6th or 7th time in my life and guess how long it took me: Slightly more than one minute!

I estimate that I will have this process down to 10 seconds or less by the time I hit the ripe old age of 100! I have become a flapper guru. The guy who has no skills when it comes to plumbing is now an "expert."

What is the point of this story? The process of learning about money, specifically about how to invest it, is not so easy when we are first exposed to the new information. It seems difficult and it takes us a long time to figure it out. We might feel rather dumb as we fumble our way through the process (we all start at the beginning).

This process is unfamiliar and strange and that should not surprise us. That is expected and normal and it should not stop us from continuing down that road toward becoming the informed and successful investor as we slowly, but surely, accumulate knowledge and the habits that we use to act on what we know.

We must stick with it and keep repeating what we have learned as the information starts to "sink in" and the habits become second nature to us. The process will become easier over time (just like that flapper became easier to me). Finally, the day will come when we have formed our habits so deeply based on what we know that we don't even think twice about how we invest our money. It becomes second nature. It becomes "easy."

The difficult flapper problem becomes the simple replacement that we do while watching a football game that is being reflected off the mirror in the bathroom! The difficult becomes very simple once we know what we are doing and it is repeated time and time again.

Don't be afraid to tackle the difficult world of investing. Strange as it may be, it will become less strange as your depth of knowledge becomes greater. Years from now, you will look back and wonder what all the fuss was about. You will see investing as relatively simple once the basics are understood. You will have become an expert investor!

"As a single footstep will not make a path on the earth, so a single thought will not make a pathway in the mind. To make a deep physical path, we walk again and again. To make a deep mental path, we must think over and over the kind of thoughts we wish to dominate our lives."

- **Henry David Thoreau**

10

THE UNDERDOG

Do you root for the underdog when watching a sporting event or some other type of competition? I do. I like to see the "little guy" beat the big strong guy. I enjoy watching someone defy logic as they triumph over what appears to be very big obstacles. That whole David and Goliath story really resonates with me. I would venture to say at different stages in our lives, we have all played the underdog a time or two.

This chapter discusses an underdog as it relates to becoming the wise and successful investor. The underdog in the world of investing is the average person like you and me who attempts to grow our investments while avoiding the many pitfalls. There are a great deal of people, companies, and systems working against us and yet, we keep fighting to make our way toward a successful financial future.

There are many people out there who discount the abilities of the individual in achieving a high return on their investments. They tell us we aren't smart enough. They tell us our emotional state will sabotage our plan. They even tell us to hand over our responsibility to others. I say hogwash! You and I can do this. It just takes a bit of stubbornness, education and self-reflection as you find your way.

We can educate ourselves, and that is why you are reading these words. We can learn to harness our emotions, which is why we learn to understand and deal with our fears and lock up our greed whenever it shows its ugly self. Finally, we know that most of the financial industry spends their days trying to figure out ways to squeeze every dollar out of us, not add to our kitty. We know this is on us. This is our responsibility. The underdog can have his day in the sun!

Make no mistake, though. We are the underdog. The system is not built for us, but we have people on our side and they have been there for quite some time. John Bogle, the creator of the first publicly traded index fund, is the first name that comes to mind.

Mr. Bogle has been a champion of the little guy for quite some time. He was telling us we could do it before most (including myself) believed him. He was right, but it took some encouragement from Mr. Bogle for the average person to "take the plunge."

I took that leap of faith well over two decades ago and educated myself on the world of investing. Thanks to people like John Bogle, that leap of faith was rewarded and not with just money. I was rewarded with a sense of empowerment. I could do it and I did. I am one of the best investors in America and so are many of my fellow underdogs. The little guy has triumphed!

Now please don't think my ego has run amok. I am not making the case that I am smarter than everyone else and I know where the markets are going. I don't and I don't have to. What I need to do is save consistently into no-load index funds that diversify me all over the world at the lowest possible costs into negative correlated assets that keep the ship upright when storms appear out of nowhere.

If some of those terms sound foreign to you, don't sweat it. Keep reading, keep learning, and believe in the underdog. John Bogle believes in you. I believe in you. Now it's time for YOU to believe in YOU.

"The remarkable thing is we have a choice everyday regarding the attitude we will embrace for that day. We cannot change our past...we cannot change the fact that people will act in a certain way. We cannot change the inevitable. The only thing we can do is play on the one string we have, and that is our attitude. I am convinced that life is 10 % what happens to me and 90 % of how I react to it..."

- **Chuck Swindoll**

11

CHECKMATE!

Have you ever played chess? I believe this board game can explain the game of investing in ways that are better than throwing a bunch of numbers at you. Chess can teach us how to become a great investor. Don't worry if you are not familiar with the game (chess or investing). This chapter will introduce you to both and how you can succeed.

The game of chess involves a bunch of funny looking pieces that are allowed to make many different types of moves throughout the game. Sometimes you are allowed to move straight ahead. Sometimes you are allowed to move diagonally. Sometimes you are allowed to move one up and two over or vice versa. It looks pretty crazy to those who don't understand the rules of the game. Investing isn't much different.

The game of investing requires a person to find the right investments, own the right percentage of those investments, and then reap the highest return AFTER costs. Your opponent (the financial services industry) tries to outmaneuver you throughout the process. This can seem quite intimidating to those who are uninformed on how this game of investing is played. It looks like a crazy game with a bunch of moving pieces that make no sense. Are you starting to see the comparisons?

So how do you win in the game of chess? First, you understand how the game is played and that takes some time as you educate yourself thoroughly on the subject. Next, you start playing the game with a close eye toward the finish. The winner is the person who captures the opponent's king. You have to start thinking 2, 3, and maybe 4 moves ahead when trying to design a plan to win. Winning at chess requires a person to plan ahead based on their present moves. Investing is no different.

The informed and successful investor knows that winning the game (capturing the highest return after costs) requires a true education from independent sources and an ability to see multiple moves beyond where they currently are (always think long-term when playing the game of investing). To those who learn how to play this game well, great rewards can be had.

I am going to show you how to play the game of investing. I have played it for 31 years with different degrees of success along the way. I started out as a novice (like we all do). I only thought about one move at a time and because of that, my opponent (the "helpers") kept kicking my butt. I learned from these experiences and my game improved.

I continued to absorb information as I found those independent sources who would guide me toward capturing those high returns after costs. Gradually, I started thinking 3 or 4 moves ahead. My mindset had changed. I had become the long-term thinker and my investment returns showed it. I started beating my opponent and I started to realize that opponent wasn't the financial industry services after all.

I learned that I was playing a game with myself. This was a revelation at the time, but I came to understand the value of knowing who the true opponent was, it was me!

Once I acknowledged the real threat, I set out to not necessarily win, but to understand. Worlds started to appear where there was darkness. This might be kind of difficult for some of you to accept at this moment. That's okay. Stay with me. Checkmate may follow!

"It is by going down into the abyss that we recover the treasures of life. Where you stumble, there lies your treasure."

- **Joseph Campbell**

Stage II

INVESTORS

BEWARE!

12

THE MINEFIELD

To become a wise and successful investor, you will be required to maneuver your way through a minefield. A minefield? This minefield I am describing is very dangerous for the individual investor, and without knowledge of it and understanding of the forces working against you, there will be casualties.

I want to help you avoid being a casualty AND help you find your way out of the darkness and into a bright financial future. I have walked this path, and I am coming back to help you do the same. I know where the land mines are located and I will help you avoid them and the people who lay them out strategically to capture you and your money. It's dangerous out there!

This section of the book, which is by far the biggest section, is designed to help you see the land mines that could ruin you and your portfolio of investments. This could be difficult. Just like land mines, there are plenty of hidden costs with your investments that can blow up in your face without even knowing they were there. Knowledge can help you avoid poor returns and unexpected expenses.

The financial services industry serves their needs, not yours.

This industry has placed themselves between you and the investments you will need to grow your money over time. You need to go around that industry, their "helpers," and their grubby little hands that keep ending up in YOUR pockets.

You are dealing with a well-funded industry that spends a great deal of money every year marketing themselves as your protector and savior. They are neither your protector nor your savior. They are your enemy in most cases. Once you fully grasp that idea, you are ready to start finding your way around their embedded minefield.

What will it take to maneuver your way through this minefield? It will take a complete education on the current state of the financial industry. Your ability to act on that information will serve you well for many decades to come. There is a path that you can follow toward becoming the wise and successful investor. That path will get you through the minefield.

Over the next thirty or so chapters, you will be provided a great deal of negative commentary on the current investing landscape. Don't let that get you down. There is plenty wrong with the system right now, but there is plenty right as well. I will help you see what is right and assist you toward getting on that path toward financial success. Issues are identified and solutions are provided.

Thanks to a guy by the name of John Bogle, there is a light at the end of the tunnel for the average investor. Stay with me throughout this journey and I will show you that light.

"Brokers and investment advisors cannot beat market returns over the long term. They talk the talk, but they can't walk the walk. There are hundreds of academic studies that demonstrate this fact conclusively. If investors knew this, they wouldn't use these brokers or advisors. But the securities industry, assisted by the financial media, perpetuates the myth that they are able to beat the markets consistently over the long term, and they hide the data that demonstrate conclusively that this simply is not true. Investors of all stripes lose billions of dollars a year because they don't understand that there is an easy, sure-fire way to achieve market returns without using brokers or investment advisors."

- **Daniel Solin**, *The Smartest Investment Book You'll Ever Read*

13

WALL STREET

Some people associate Wall Street with the actual companies that make up the markets. That's a mistake. They are not the same and they should not be seen as the same. Wall Street is made up of people who make a living trading in markets all over the world. Markets are made up of securities that ultimately go up and down on a daily basis based on their assessed value (what Wall Street gauges as their current value). This short-term valuation can be and is, wrong much of the time.

What is assessed value and why should you care? That is where Wall Street and its many analysts add their input and predictions. These well informed men and women crunch the numbers that come from the publicly traded companies. They look into their crystal ball, and then they make assessments on the direction of individual securities, sectors in the economy, and large markets that stretch all over the world. Sometimes they are right and many times they are wrong.

Predicting the future is hard, and that is why so many people fail at it. You and I don't have to play that game, and we should not spend time around people who try to predict the future. This is why we should own markets (stocks and bonds) all over the world while ignoring the daily gyrations that are caused by those "psychics."

This is a revelation to many people when they read what I just wrote. Ignore those large and famous firms on Wall Street. Ignore those "helpers" who work for those large and famous firms. Ignore their commercials as they market themselves and their products to an uninformed audience. Ignore them all and instead, own markets all over the world at the lowest possible cost.

This can be a very empowering feeling. You can ignore Wall Street and the daily ups and downs of the markets. You can ignore everyone in the media who talks about the daily ups and downs of the market.

You can ignore friends, family, and strangers who pop into your life and stress over the daily ups and downs of the markets. They can all be ignored because what they have to say doesn't matter. That's right. What they say has no relevance to the long-term value of securities.

What matters are the earnings and dividends your stocks (equities) pay you based on the growth of those businesses. What matters is the interest your bonds (fixed income) pay you based on their maturities and quality. Those are things that truly matter, not predictions about the future of a security or the ramblings of others based on what they see as the future of one market or another.

Learning to identify what actually matters and what doesn't matter in the world of investing can set you free! You can ignore almost all of what you hear (and see) as you diversify your investments all over the world in a few inexpensive index mutual funds (more on those later) that own thousands of individual stocks and bonds. The future belongs to those individuals who see the truth through the clouds of chaos.

"As an investor, what should you do about forecasts—forecasts of the stock market, forecasts of interest rates, forecasts of the economy? Answer: Nothing. You can save time, anxiety, and money by ignoring all market forecasts."

- **Charles Ellis and Burton Malkiel,** *The Elements of Investing*

14

THE FINANCIAL SERVICES INDUSTRY

The financial services industry makes a lot of money off the uninformed investor. I mean a LOT of money! Billions of dollars every year are siphoned off the individual and institutional investor's return on investment. What does the investor get in return? Less money earned on their investments. A LOT less!

So who am the "helpers" that I want you to avoid? Stockbrokers, fee-based financial advisors, and life insurance agents are the primary culprits. These "experts" are sent out to "help" you, but that is not what is actually happening. So what is exactly going on?

It's really not that complicated. Many of these smart people work for large firms, banks, and insurance companies. Those large institutions have created a business model that pulls in large amounts of money each and every day to them and their "helpers." They promise alpha (return beyond the markets). They promise safety. They even promise some type of psychic ability as they try to predict the future of markets.

So how do they do collectively? Horribly! They reduce your total return. They don't add to it. Think about that for a moment. You pay these smart people to reduce your returns. Does that sound like a good idea? Hell no, and yet it continues to happen year after year, and decade after decade.

Why? We are easily influenced by their marketing campaigns, pretty outfits, credentials, big buildings, and "amazing" predictions on what they are going to do and where the markets are headed. We pay for something we don't get. There is a better way.

I have identified the problem and I promise you, it is very real. The question is, "What can you do about it?" Become your own financial advisor, that's what. When you do, you discard the stockbroker, the fee-based financial advisor and the life insurance agent. You don't need them, and you certainly cannot afford them.

Does it scare you to fire those "helpers" and their employers as you take over the job of investing yourself? Don't sweat it; there is a solution to that understandable concern.

You can reduce that fear through education, specifically a financial education on investing your money and taking control of your life. DO NOT step away from that fear. Step into it and you will see those fears gradually shrink away as you build on your financial education.

This might be where you start to think, "What does Finley know?" I know what five Nobel Laureates have taught me. I know what Charles Ellis and Burton Malkiel have taught me. I know what William Bernstein, David Swensen, Daniel Solin, Larry Swedroe and Rick Ferri have taught me. I certainly know what John Bogle has taught me. Finally, I know what the greatest investor of our time, Warren Buffett, has taught me.

Here is a question for you. Are you going to learn from these true independent experts or your local stockbroker, fee-based financial advisor, and/or life insurance agent? That is a pretty silly question in my mind. Learn from the best and the brightest. Join OUR team!

"The investment business is a giant scam. Most people think they can find managers who can outperform, but most people are wrong. I will say that 85 to 90 percent of managers fail to match their benchmarks. Because managers have fees and incur transaction costs, you know that in the aggregate they are deleting value. You want to keep your fees low. That means avoiding the most hyped but expensive funds, in favor of low-cost index funds."

- **Jack Meyer,** former president of the Harvard Management Company

Markets vs. The Average Investor

The numbers below were taken from a DALBAR study, Quantitative Analysis of Investor Behavior (QAIB, 03/2010). The market returns reflect a period that spans two decades in which one was very good for stocks and one was very good for bonds. This includes the 2008 debacle in the stock market.

The total return of stocks and bonds would have been quite good for the investor who would have owned the large stock and bond markets throughout this time period. This example illustrates that buying and holding your investments works!

The stark difference in returns also tells us a lot about how the financial services industry skims off our return and how poor the individual investors are at timing the market.

Time Period

1 Jan 1990 to 31 Dec 2009

S&P 500 Index	Average Stock Investor
8.20%	3.17%

Barclays Bond Index	Average Bond Investor
7.01%	1.02%

15

THE STOCKBROKER

I laugh every time I read about stockbrokers. They are an interesting group of people. The average stockbroker may study for a couple of weeks so they can pass the Series 7 and Series 6 tests and maybe a couple more so they can trade futures and other products. Once they pass those tests, voila, they are investment professionals!

You should avoid ALL stockbrokers.

These types of people are not in the business of changing the world through performing good deeds and helping grandma cross the road. They are in the business to make a boat load of money and do it as fast as they possibly can (Google "Jordan Belfort" to learn more). How do they accomplish that? They get people like you and me to trade securities like stocks and bonds as often as possible. That is how they make money!

Stockbrokers should be on your "avoid at all times" list. They are detrimental to your wealth, health, and general disposition. They suck life from you with promises that are empty from the start. They are not your buddies, and they are certainly not investment experts. They hold no fiduciary responsibility, which means, they are going to do what is best for them and their firms (much of the time brokers are pushing individual securities because they are told to push one over another).

And yet, thousands of people use stockbrokers to make trades and use them as advisors when considering their next move with their money. That is insane! NEVER listen to a stockbroker when he or she is passing out advice on investing. They exist simply because of the inability of some to see through the illusion of expertise.

Keep this in mind: Every time you make a trade, there is someone on the other end either buying or selling, and that someone else is usually a professional and/or a computer that has access to information that you and I will never have.

We are the last to know, and here is where I am talking about the people who play fairly (there are plenty of people who cheat and trade on inside information, Google "Martha Stewart" or "Raj Rajaratnam" for examples). Not only should you avoid a stockbroker, but also you should avoid individual stocks every step of the way.

There is no reason in the world that you and I should by picking individual stocks. It is a loser's game from the get-go. Buying and selling individual stocks puts your money at great risk of loss, and you do it because you or your "guy" thinks it is a great move. It's not, and it never was. That is greed and ego talking. Nothing more.

Take your hard earned money and invest in no-load stock and bond index mutual funds that own thousands of individual securities all over the world at the lowest possible cost. Your risk of loss drops dramatically as you own thousands of securities rather than a handful.

It is time to become the informed investor. You put your greed, your ego, and even your fear aside as you watch your investments GROW and GROW and GROW with that wonderful thing called compound interest. Awake to the possibilities!

"There are two kinds of investors, be they large or small: Those who don't know where the market is headed, and those who don't know that they don't know. Then again, there is a third type of investor, the investment professional who indeed knows that he or she doesn't know, but whose livelihood depends upon appearing to know."

- **William Bernstein**, *The Intelligent Asset Allocator*

16

THE LIFE INSURANCE AGENT

Many people invest their money using life insurance products. Here is a short list: equity-indexed annuities, fixed rate annuities, variable annuities, whole life insurance, variable life insurance, universal life insurance and indexed universal life insurance. You should avoid them all! Yep, investing in life insurance products using your local life insurance agent is a BIG mistake.

Why? Life insurance products are loaded with high commissions and high yearly fees that help fund that industry and pay the salaries to the agents they send out to sell their products. Who pays those commissions and high fees? The individual who buys those expensive products covers those costs either directly or indirectly. Just because you don't get a bill does not mean you are not paying. Let's take a look.

Life insurance products pay big fat commissions to the agents who sell them (100% in the first year in some cases). Those products lock up your money for many years (seven to ten years is pretty normal) as you are charged high yearly fees to pay those big fat commissions to the agents and large salaries to the big shots at the corporate office. Does that sound like a winning situation? It's not for us. It is for them.

If you pull your money out early, you will end up paying big surrender fees on life insurance products that protect those expected commissions, fees, and salaries. Once again, we are seeing a business model that has been created, which is very good for the industry and its "helpers," but not so much for you and me. A financial education can stop this from happening as you learn how the game is played!

You should avoid investing with life insurance products, whether you are dealing with annuities or cash value policies that provide some type of life insurance benefit that is also tied to an investment. If you need life insurance, buy term life at a place like accuquote.com or term4sale.com.

When you invest with life insurance products, you end up with low returns, less than expected results and promises that were not fulfilled in many, many cases. Why then, do so many people invest using life insurance products? It starts with a great marketing plan; it's followed with a barrage of advertising, and it closes with talented salespeople locking your money up using the pitch of guaranteed returns.

Now let's identify the truth. If you have to spend millions of dollars every year to market your products, maybe your products aren't that great. If it takes commercial after commercial to convince people it's the right way to go, maybe it's not. Finally, if you have to promise guaranteed returns to entice people to give up control of their money, maybe a guarantee isn't worth what you think it is. Basically, you are guaranteed low returns with high yearly fees. Is that what you want? I don't think so.

Here is the truth that you won't see in any commercial. The clients (you and me) end up paying for it all. We pay for the marketing. We pay for the advertisements and, yes we pay for the guarantees with those high yearly fees and surrender penalties. We also pay those large salaries and bonuses to the big shots in the skyscrapers. Avoid life insurance products and the agents who sell them. It's that simple.

"Beware of brokers and insurance agents eager to escort your cash to another annuity. Investors get switched from one mediocre annuity to another all the time because brokers receive healthy commissions every time they convince someone to jump."

- **Daniel Solin,** *The Smartest Retirement Book You'll Ever Read*

17

THE FEE-BASED ADVISOR

I am a true believer in the individual taking control of their financial situation and becoming their own financial advisor, but I realize some people are just not ready to take that responsibility on or they are not capable for one reason or another. This chapter highlights the people you need to avoid when seeking help.

There are many "helpers" in the financial services industry and most of them are fee-based salespeople. What does that mean? They earn money in different ways, and one of them almost always involves commissions/loads as well as kick backs from the companies whose products they sell.

Those commissions/loads cause a conflict of interest. Basically, those fee-based advisors end up working for others rather than for YOU. Incentives are baked into the system, and they push those fee-based advisors to sell expensive products that are not in your best interest.

Your local fee-based advisor will not tell you that they are working for someone else, but they are, rest assured. Informed investors know this and have known this for quite some time. You need to avoid fee-based advisors if you want your investments to grow over time. It really is that simple, and the sooner in life you learn that, the better off you will be.

Here is some bad news. Most people use **fee-based salespeople**. Why is that? Most investors don't understand this issue AND it is hard to find **fee-only advisors** (discussed in a later chapter) because there are so few of them. Why is that? There is a lot of money to be made with the fee-based business model. Hmmm....

That business model was built by the financial industry to make money for them and their "helpers" by skimming off your return before they give you what is left. Take a moment and think about that. These salespeople are stuck in a business model that exploits the individual investor as they make their firms a great deal of money. They feed off the ignorance of the average individual investor. Those fee-based advisors fund many retirement accounts, just not yours!

You need to stay away from fee-based "helpers" in the financial industry. When I say stay away, I mean RUN away! Do not go to their free dinners. Do not go to their office. Do not have a drink with them. Do not work out with them! Avoid them at all costs!

How do you identify one of these types of advisors? It's pretty simple when you know the right questions to ask. Here are a few that will help you figure out who you are dealing with.

- How do they get paid?
- Who pays them and how much?
- What is their investment philosophy?
- Do they attempt to time the market?
- Do they attempt to identify winning securities?

If they say you don't pay them, run away! If they hem and haw without giving you a straight answer, run away! If they change the subject, run away! The bottom line: If you don't get a straight answer to your questions in a short period of time, leave quickly and don't look back!

"Wall Street, with its army of brokers, analysts, and advisers funneling trillions of dollars into mutual funds, hedge funds, and private equity funds, is an elaborate fraud."

- **Michael Lewis**, Author of *Liar's Poker*

High Cost vs. Low Cost

Below, you will see fifty years of compounding costs on a $10,000 lump-sum investment earning a 9.4% annual return (that matches a historical return where you held 80% in stocks and 20% in bonds and cash). Note: No other money was added to the account.

The load demonstrates a yearly cost of 3 percent, based on commissions paid to the salesperson and fees paid to the financial institution (this could include cash-value life insurance policies, annuities, and managed load mutual funds to name just a few).

The no-load demonstrates an industry average of fees paid to no-load mutual funds managed by people who spend their days buying and selling a lot (no commissions, no loads, just fees).

The index shows the fees you would pay in a portfolio of index funds. The numbers represent what you lose by investing with "smart people" versus index funds. The choice should be clear.

$10,000 in 50 years

Type	Cost	You lose it	You keep it
Load	3.0%	$689,323	$193,706
No-Load	1.5%	$468,836	$414,193
Index	.09%	$39,278	$843,751

18

THE MEDIA

What you hear coming from the television and most media sources regarding investing is CRAP the vast majority of time. Actually, it's worse than crap. At least you can shovel up crap and throw it in the garbage to get rid of it. Media-based crap seems to multiply!

What they are providing you on television is entertainment and nothing more in most cases. The pundits try to predict future market ups and downs as if they actually know where those markets are headed. They don't! You would be wise to ignore almost everything you hear regarding the world of investing when it comes from media sources.

Why? The media is there to grab your attention. They need people with strong opinions to come into your living room and make their case one way or the other regarding future market returns. Those "experts" have 24 hours a day to fill. They don't have to be right, and most of the time they are not. When they do get something right, it's almost always luck (or possibly cheating). DO NOT waste your time listening to these blowhards.

Why do so many people listen to the media darlings? Those people on television look rather wise for one thing. They have business degrees, finance degrees, credentials that show they passed a test, and they are on television, for goodness sake. They must be knowledgeable, right?

Just because they can speak the language of money does not mean you should listen to them. Any time you see someone prognosticating about the future, turn that dial! Would you listen to some psychic tell you how to invest your money? I hope you answered no to that question. Well, those folks on television are playing psychics dressed in pretty outfits.

Here is where it can get difficult. I realize that it makes sense to listen to these people as they are identified as the experts. I get that, but they are not the experts. The true experts spend little time on television. Why is that? What they have to say is not overly exciting. The media likes exciting and provocative people. Let's try an experiment. You tell me what media source would invite someone on to make these honest statements.

- The average investor should ignore the media.
- The average investor should avoid stockbrokers.
- The average investor should avoid life insurance agents.
- The average investor should avoid fee-based financial advisors.
- The average investor should learn from experts NOT on TV.
- The average investor should own no-load index mutual funds.
- The average investor should invest at the lowest possible cost.
- The average investor should rebalance once a year or so.
- I have no earthly idea what direction the market is heading.

What do you think? Would they invite anyone on to make those statements? I don't think so. It's just not very exciting, and the media sources need exciting! Here is the bottom line: The media provides entertainment, not education. Never forget that.

"The single greatest threat to your financial well-being is the hyperactive broker or advisor. The second greatest threat to your financial well-being is the false belief that you can trade on your own, online or otherwise, and attempt to beat the markets by engaging in stock picking or market timing. Finally, the third greatest threat to your financial well-being is paying attention too much of the financial media, which is often engaged in nothing more than "financial pornography." This conduct generates ad revenues for them and losses for investors who rely on the misinformation that is their daily grist."

- **Daniel Solin,** *The Smartest Investment Book You'll Ever Read*

19

THE GREAT MAN

Finding the Great Man when it comes to investing is easy AFTER the results are reported. It is virtually impossible to identify that person BEFORE the game is played. Feel free to replace the Great Man with the Great Woman. It is one in the same.

Let's take a moment and look at the greatest investor of our time, Warren Buffett, the "Oracle of Omaha." Mr. Buffett has produced amazing results over his lifetime, and I am impressed with his record just as you should be. So why don't we just do what he does? Because we can't!

Mr. Buffett buys and sells securities less often than you and I change cars! He buys great companies after his extensive research and talents tell him what the future may hold for those great companies. Charlie Monger (his right-hand man) provides a sounding board throughout the process. Is Charlie your close, personal friend? I doubt it.

Once Mr. Buffett buys a large share in company stock, he tends to get very involved in that business. This may include sitting on their board of directors and guiding them toward making future decisions that affect the bottom line of that business. It has worked very, very well for Mr. Buffett and his Berkshire Hathaway shareholders. I commend him, but that does not mean we can do the same.

You and I have nowhere near the influence that someone like Warren Buffett will have, and that is a supreme understatement, to say the least. You and I am not Warren Buffett, and we should not try to invest like Warren Buffett. I hope I have made that point perfectly clear by now, but there is more to this story, as they say.

You and I should not try to find the next Great Man. Is he out there? Sure he is, but no one knows who that is going to be. Nobody knew who Warren Buffett was once upon a time. I would venture to say that most people just saw him as some hick from Omaha who liked cheeseburgers and Coke. Wall Street surely scoffed at this "novice."

It is ludicrous to think you and I could pick out the next Warren Buffett. Many people try. Many people also attempt to mimic what Mr. Buffett does when he invests the money he manages. This is a big mistake, and you need to know that.

Many advisors, friends, and family will cite that Warren Buffett did not make his fortune by investing in index funds. They are right, but they are missing the point. We are not Warren Buffett. We should not compare ourselves to him, and we should not try to be like him.

We SHOULD listen to Warren Buffett's advice when it comes to how the average person should invest. He tells us to use index funds. Here are three key points to remember when anyone starts talking about the Great Man, whoever that might be in any given time period.

- DO NOT try to be Warren Buffett.

- DO NOT try to invest like Warren Buffett.

- DO NOT try to identify the next Warren Buffett.

"… Given the professional culture of the financial community, it is not surprising that large numbers of individuals in that world believe themselves to be among the chosen few who can do what they believe others cannot."

- **Daniel Kauneman**, Nobel Laureate in Economics

20

THE GREAT STOCK

Have you ever heard somebody talk about their regrets in not buying a great company when it was just starting out? You know, you hear things like, "If only I had bought Wal-Mart, Microsoft, Facebook, or Apple when they were young and very small. I would have made a fortune."

Is that true? Could be, or maybe they are not seeing the very big downside. When we spend our days trying to find the next Great Stock, we could also end up with a stock whose company goes bankrupt and we are stuck with empty pockets.

Thousands and thousands of people spend their days trying to find that one Great Stock that will "hit it big." They buy penny stocks and small companies you have never heard of, as they search all over the world for that "diamond in the rough." Finding the next Apple will make them rich, or so they think. This kind of thinking and action should be avoided.

Let's take a look at Apple. Most people today would love to have owned Apple when it was first offered to the public in December 1980. Millionaires were created overnight. If you were one of them, you certainly could be very wealthy today, but there is more to the story as we start to explore this illusion of finding the Great Stock.

Apple was a company started by a hippy and a nerd. (I use those words in describing how many people might have described Steve Jobs and Steve Wozniak at that time.) Those gentlemen had almost no sense of how to run a company, and they had very little capital. They were working out of a garage, and in many cases, they were trying to do something that had never been done. Does that sound like a company you want to own?

Years later when Apple got bigger, they fired Steve Jobs and came very, very close to bankruptcy. The stock fell to $7 in 2002, and many people thought it would keep falling. No one was clamoring for Apple stock in 2002. As a matter of fact, there were many people bailing out before the "ship sinks."

What point am I making? The informed investor does not try to seek out the Great Stock. There is no way to know whether some hick in Arkansas is going to create one of the largest companies in the world (many people saw Sam Walton as a hick when he was building his Wal-Mart empire). There is no way to identify when some kid in his Harvard college dorm room is going to create something that might change the world (see Bill Gates and Mark Zuckerberg for examples).

Trying to find the needle in the haystack is a fool's errand, and the informed investor knows this and avoids it. The great company is buried in a large pile of bad companies. Successful companies do not necessarily make for great stocks to own, and bad companies can actually end up being very good stocks to own in some cases (more on that later in the Fama and French chapter).

Finding the Great Stock is irrelevant to the informed investor. They know that successful investing requires education, broad diversification, a focus on cost and tax management, and maybe most importantly, they know that chasing the Great Stock is a sure-fire way to end up with nothing. Let someone else chase the illusion of the Great Stock.

"It's bad enough that you have to take market risk. Only a fool takes on the additional risk of doing yet more damage by failing to diversify properly with his or her nest egg. Avoid the problem--buy a well-run index fund and own the whole market."

- **William Bernstein**, *The Four Pillars of Investing*

21

EMOTIONS

Emotions can cause you to make some really bad decisions when it comes to investing. Over the next few chapters I will be discussing this issue in more detail. I will also attempt to help you deal with the issue in the real world where life is not always so easy.

Here are a few things I would like you to know. The best investors take emotion out of their decision-making. They focus on the research and the facts, while staying rational in a very irrational and psychologically disturbing world. Basically, they stay grounded when others are losing their minds AND their money.

Your emotions can make or break you when it comes to investing. The fewer emotional decisions you make with your money, the better off you are going to be. How can you deal with emotions when they are a big part of what makes you human? Here are three ways you can better understand this issue and how to deal with it.

(1) Identify the fact that emotions play a big part in our daily lives and rather than deny them, learn to understand them.

(2) Acknowledge that emotions can cause us to behave in detrimental ways that will have a far-reaching impact on our future.

(3) Learn to compare what we feel to the facts at hand before making decisions with our money.

There is a whole field of study that deals with the psychological decision-making of human beings. I am not going to get in-depth on this issue, partly because there is no need to, and partly because it can get pretty deep and confusing. Saying that, there is certainly important information we can learn from the world of psychology and behavioral economics.

Here are a few basics that might help you in better understanding YOU. Human beings are conditioned to do many things based on rewards and punishment. We strive to receive those rewards and try to avoid the punishments. Maybe we do these things consciously or subconsciously, but rest assured, our behaviors follow after our feelings just like a young puppy follows after his mother.

It's not always peaceful when dealing with our emotions. You might even see this as a war between the emotional side of you and the rational side. Try to avoid fighting that war. Fighting your emotional state will get you nowhere. I recommend you make peace with your emotions, while acknowledging them.

Learning to understand your emotions and then adapting them into your investing life can be very beneficial. The successful investor accomplishes this as they dig deep into who they are to better understand why they do what they do.

Know thyself.

"There is a lot riding on the decisions you make. As you make those decisions, don't trip yourself. Investors with no knowledge, no plan, no discipline, no benchmarks, and no clue have no chance. They would be only slightly worse off to take their money to the dog track or play lotto. It's hard work to build and implement a superior portfolio. But not nearly as difficult as maintaining that portfolio through thick and thin so that you reach your financial goals. The temptation to do something truly stupid can seem almost overwhelming. Train yourself to resist it."

- **Frank Armstrong III**, *The Informed Investor*

22

FEAR

Fear can stop you from investing. It can also sabotage your efforts if you are investing. Fear is one of the many emotions you will have to harness if you want to be the wise and successful investor. Notice the word "harness", rather than "eliminate."

You cannot eliminate fear from your investing life and you should not try. What you can do is educate yourself to reduce your fears throughout your journey toward understanding this rather abstract idea of investing wisely. This is a really big deal and without some real self-awareness, this emotion could take over your life and take you to places you do not want to go. Let's take a look.

Many people do not invest their money because they are fearful that they will "lose it all." They see investing as gambling. When you are uninformed it is natural to see investing as gambling. Fear overwhelms these kinds of people causing them to stay out of any market that goes up and down throughout the year.

Many others do invest their money, but at any sign of trouble, they attempt to move their money out of the risky investments like stocks and into the low-risk cash accounts. This gives these kinds of people a sense of control, but it shouldn't. Moving your money around in an attempt to avoid the losses is a loser's game.

I am not trying to discount your fears. I know they are real, but in many cases, they are nothing more than negative scripts running through your head. You must learn to identify this negative chatter when it pops in your head and see it for what it is.

Fear is that emotion that tells you to run every time something scary comes along. That is a good thing when a grizzly bear is coming your way. It is a bad thing when you are trying to capture a return on your money that exceeds the annual inflation rate. Let's see what you can do to deal with this matter realistically and without denying the reality of this emotion.

Can you lose all of your money when investing? Yes, if you put all of your money in one stock or bond. That security could be worth nothing if the company or organization goes bankrupt. That's why you don't put all your money in one stock or bond.

You put your money in thousands and thousands of stocks and bonds, which will diversify you over many parts of the world. Broad diversification can reduce this fear. The Total Stock Market Index Fund at Vanguard owns about 4,000 individual stocks that diversify you all over the world (many of the large companies in America make half or more of their money from overseas markets). That is safety in numbers.

What about the fear of loss, which causes you to move money out of risky assets? It fails miserably in most cases. By moving money around, the average investor loses most of the market gains and ends up getting whacked by the real risk of inflation as their money sits in the "safe" cash accounts waiting for the "right time" to get back in the market.

Here it is. Fear is not your friend when it comes to investing. Education combined with a plan that you stick to can push those fears aside. This will ultimately increase your returns over time.

Know thyself.

"According to a recent survey of 1,000 investors, there's a 51% chance that in any given year, the U.S. stock market might drop by one-third. And yet, based on history, the odds that U.S. stocks will lose a third of their value in a given year are only around 2%. The real risk is not that the stock market will have a meltdown, but that inflation will raise your cost of living and erode your savings."

- **Jason Zweig**, *Your Money & Your Brain*

23

EGO

Allowing your ego to dominate your investing decisions can be detrimental to your future success. Men tend to have a bigger problem than women on this issue, but anyone can be susceptible to it simply because they are human. We all have an ego and learning to understand it and harness it can make a big difference in our future. This matter tends to get a bit complicated so stay with me as I explore it in detail.

The ego we all have can cloud our judgment when investing our money. It can force us into making poor decisions simply because we "know" what is the right thing to do at any particular time based on what we hear, see and possibly even feel (think intuition). Here is where it gets complicated and a bit odd.

It is important for you to develop a good sense of self. Mom and Dad would be proud of you. Increasing self-esteem and confidence can make a positive difference in your life, but it can be dangerous with regard to investing.

If you allow your ego to drive your investing decision-making, you could end up with poor returns, high costs, high taxes and high levels of stress. I seriously doubt anyone wants that.

The wise and successful investors keep their egos in check as they push aside the idea that they know what the future of markets or individual stocks might do. They throw up their hands and say, "I have no earthly idea what direction the market is headed." That does not mean you are uninformed. It simply means you accept the fact that you don't know.

To be informed is to know that YOU DON'T KNOW. If that sounds strange to you, welcome aboard. It sounds strange to me as well, but it's worth repeating. It can be very useful when you come to the realization that you don't know and you don't have to know.

It is extremely important that you understand that smart investing eliminates the negative affects that come with letting the ego drive our decision-making. It releases that part of your mind that believes you are required to know the next move in the market. Simply acknowledge that you don't, and you have conquered the ego (for the moment).

The informed and successful investors put their egos aside as they invest in markets all over the world without trying to pick "the right one." They focus on broad diversification, costs, and passive investing (buy and hold), rather than timing or expertise from the "experts."

The wise investors focus on education above all else. They develop a plan and stick to it through good times and bad. They realize the ego is an impediment to the process and works against them much more than working for them. It ultimately reduces the final return when it is allowed to rear its ugly head.

Know thyself.

"Before acting on seemingly valuable information, ask yourself why you believe that information is not already incorporated into prices. Only incremental insight has value. Capturing incremental insight is difficult because there are so many smart, highly motivated analysts doing the same research. If you hear recommendations on CNBC or from your broker or read them in Barron's, the market already knows the information it is based on. It has no value."

- **Larry Swedroe,** *The Quest for Alpha*

24

GREED

Greed is not your friend when it comes to investing. I know some people think it is and they think that investing requires a person to think in greedy ways, but I see no evidence of that. Greed is an emotion that must be controlled if you want to be a successful investor.

The wise investors take their greed and stick it in the closet and lock the door. It has no place in your investing life. The earlier that you do this, the better off you are going to be. Greed is a monster that crushes not only your portfolio, but also your soul. Let's see how it happens.

Greed causes many people to try to "hit it big." The investors who allow greed to enter their life chase after investments with the idea that they are going to get rich FAST. Here are a list of possibilities that tend to bring out the greed in many: Penny stocks, hot new ideas, IPOs (initial public offerings), and in some cases, gold and silver. Here is the truth. Greed will reduce your wealth rather than increase it.

Greed can easily pop up and change the way you invest your money. Let's take a look at an example. You see and hear about a business that is going to revolutionize the world and in a few days they will be on Wall Street launching their IPO. This new business is amazing and if you get on board early, you could be RICH.

They are starting out at a price of $20 per share and a few analysts are predicting the price will go up to $60 in a week. It could be $100 in a month. It could be $200 in two months! The excitement is palpable. Everyone is talking about it. The sky is the limit, but you had better jump on board now. This train is leaving the station.

Do you buy it? That part of you that doesn't want to miss out on a "sure thing" allows the greed gene to creep into your life as it sends your mind and heart a racing. This could be your ticket to wealth!

You see yourself making a 300% profit in a few days. You are going to be rich and admired by all! They might even talk about you one day. Hell, they might even build a monument to your amazing abilities. That is a warning to you that greed has taken over your thinking. Don't let it take over your decision-making. Let's take a look at IPOs.

IPOs tend to be very poor investments. They flame out soon after becoming public. They get overhyped, over analyzed, and shoved out to the average investor once the institutional investors have had their say on the matter. That is what an informed investor knows. They see through the noise and they keep their greed controlled.

The greed gene sits quietly in all of us. It waits until the right time and then it pounces, as it sabotages not only the present, but also the future. It can screw up your life and the lives of others in many terrible ways. Google "Ivan Boesky" and "Dennis Levine" for examples.

Keep your eyes open to see this devious monster. It is always lurking. Greed can ruin you and the people you care about. Say no to greed and the misery that follows.

Know thyself.

"Let me be clear: our emotions define our humanity, what binds us to our family, friends, and neighbors. Without them, we are soulless, heartless automatons, devoid of meaning or purpose. But in the world of finance, they are death itself."

- **William Bernstein**, *The Investor's Manifesto*

25

BUY! SELL!

During many periods of time when the markets are going up, you will have people telling you to buy NOW before it's too late! On the flip side, those same people could be telling you to sell NOW before it's too late! You must learn to ignore this kind of manic behavior that reduces returns, while increasing costs and in many cases, taxes.

There are many investors who end up getting a metaphorical whiplash as they attempt to follow one guru or another and their predictions. The gurus don't know the direction of markets any better than you and I. We need to ignore these "smart" people at every turn.

Here is a dirty little secret that you need to know. Those gurus make their big money through newsletters, books, and television shows, not through successful investing. They sell you on their skill as they rake in the money based on their ability to see the future. It is critically important that you see through this charade. It's all a show!

Here is another dirty little secret. Those gurus sell the market short (invest in ways where they benefit if the market goes down) and sell the market long (use leverage to enhance their profits if the market goes up). Do you think that might influence their "recommendations?"

This has everything to do with ego, and the gurus are not lacking in ego, I can promise you that. They think they know the direction of the markets and if they can convince enough other people on that fact, their profits will go up that much more. They don't know the direction of the markets and no matter how confident they appear, you should simply reject their ridiculous predictions on the future.

So who are these gurus? I prefer not to throw names out there because I don't like getting sued for libel for telling the truth. Calling a pig a pig should be fair game, but not in our very litigious society. Saying that, here is a good way to identify a guru when you see one or hear one.

He or she tells you what the future will be in relation to any type of market in any part of the world. A guru makes the case that they are smarter than others because they have insight or knowledge that others don't (only the cheats with insider trading meet this criteria).

A guru might jump up and down on television with bells and whistles telling you to buy, buy, buy or sell, sell, sell. This type of guru is a clown and should be ignored at all times.

So what do you do when encountering one of these gurus in everyday life? Turn the channel on TV or radio, go to a different website on the Internet, turn the page when in print, or just walk out of the room when possible. Call the guru out for what he/she is, which is a fraud.

"Buy NOW" requires no action on your part. "Sell NOW" should result in the same no action response. This will reduce your costs and taxes, increase your returns, and decrease your stress. When you encounter your next guru, I recommend you run NOW.

"Every time you decide to get out of the market *or* get in, the investors you buy from or sell to are professionals. Of course, the pros are not *always* right, but how confident are you that you will be "more right" more often than they will be? What's more, market timers incur trading costs with each and every move. And unless you are managing a tax-sheltered retirement account, you will have to pay taxes every time you take a profit. Over and over, the "benefits" of market timing prove illusory."

- **Charles Ellis**, *Winning the Loser's Game*

26

THE MANAGED MUTUAL FUND

The majority of people in the United States buy and own managed mutual funds. That's a mistake. Those fee-based advisors I mentioned earlier sell managed mutual funds all of the time to their unsuspecting and uninformed clients.

Why? Managed funds bring in more revenue for everyone involved except YOU. Do you own managed funds? If you aren't sure, you probably do. Let's take a step back for a moment and define a managed mutual fund so you know what to avoid in the future.

A managed mutual fund relies on a person or a group of people to administer a mutual fund as they attempt to buy the winning securities and avoid the losing securities. These managers use all kinds of data and research as they select the "right" securities to own, while avoiding the "wrong" securities.

These individuals are quite educated on the matter of investing and they generally hold advanced finance degrees from some of the most prestigious universities throughout America. It makes sense to give your money to these smart people, right? Intuitively it might make sense, but again, it's a mistake.

Why? The vast majority of these managers consistently fail to beat the market. Why? It comes down to costs in the majority of cases. The fees (expense ratio) can easily run well over 1% per year. That is a big hurdle to overcome as they try to outsmart other smart managers who are trying to do the same thing. The market (you see this throughout all markets in the world) beats most active managers. It's that simple.

Why do so many people own managed mutual funds? The financial services industry promotes the heck out of them as they promise you alpha. What is alpha? Alpha is a return beyond the markets. Managers tout their abilities to do this, but they fail consistently over time as stated earlier. Chasing alpha is a fool's errand. Don't fall for it.

What can you do about it? Plenty is the short answer. (1) Make a commitment to avoid managed mutual funds. (2) When buying a mutual fund, select index mutual funds that capture the market return rather than trying to beat it. (3) Buy the cheapest index funds that diversify you all over the world (strive to get your yearly costs down to something close to .1%).

Do not let an advisor convince you to switch to a managed fund just because it beat its benchmark over a given period of time. What he is withholding is the majority of managed funds that failed to beat the benchmark indexes. He is picking the diamond out of the rough to try to convince you to change investments. Don't fall for it.

Past performance of managed funds has no significance when looking at future performance. Avoid the managed funds and stick with index funds that capture market returns at the lowest possible cost. Play the probabilities over the possibilities. Keep the odds in your favor.

There will be plenty more written about index funds in the coming chapters. Take your time and continue to educate yourself on the matter prior to making important decisions on what types of investments to own. The informed investor will see why index funds are the best option.

"In every mutual fund prospectus, in every sales promotional folder, and in every mutual fund advertisement (albeit in print almost too small to read), the following warning appears: "Past performance is no guarantee of future results." Believe it!"

- **Paul Samuelson**, Nobel Laureate in Economics

Managed Funds vs. Index Funds

   The numbers stated below were taken from the mutual-fund tracking agency, Morningstar. These numbers reflect how many smart money managers failed to beat their respective indexes over a fifteen-year period spanning from 1997 to 2011.

   These numbers do not reflect loads (commissions) paid to salespeople or the dead mutual funds (funds that were closed due to poor performance) that no longer exist. The failure rate of managed funds would be higher if the tombstones were included.

Percent of managers who failed to beat their index

Large-Cap Stock Mutual Funds: 84%

Mid-Cap Stock Mutual Funds: 96%

Small-Cap Stock Mutual Funds: 95%

International Stock Mutual Funds: 64%

Short-Term Bond Mutual Funds: 98%

Intermediate-Term Bond Mutual Funds: 87%

27

BEFORE OR AFTER?

A whole lot of people in the financial industry would prefer you focus on your return on investment BEFORE costs. Why? They don't really want you scrutinizing the actual costs that are incurred all along the way. That's good for them and bad for you. I want you to focus on your return on investment AFTER costs and taxes.

The after-cost returns are really the only returns that count. That's what you end up with after it's all said and done. That is what you earned once the financial industry and its helpers took their cut. This applies to all investments whether that is stocks, bonds, real estate, insurance products, land, or even precious metals. It is critical that you identify the costs if you ever want to see your investments grow over time.

When you focus on after cost-returns, you start to take a good hard look at the commissions, loads, fees, and taxes incurred as you run the gauntlet in and around Wall Street and its many "helpers."

This can be an eye-opening experience for many. It was for me. The first time I looked at what my investments were costing me, I was stunned. It also explained why my money was not growing very fast. The people between my investments and me were taking a pretty big cut. I was feeding their retirement accounts, not mine! That had to stop if I wanted to achieve some of my goals going forward.

The first thing I did was account for all of the costs. Was I paying commissions? Was I paying loads? How about ongoing fees? What about one-time fees? Who was getting this money? What were they doing to earn it? Finally, how could I reduce these costs?

I soon realized only the uninformed paid commissions and loads, and I quickly stopped. Paying loads and commissions do nothing but reduce your returns.

I tackled the fees next, and I came to realize that my managed mutual funds charged annual fees that came in close to 1.5% per year (do not underestimate how big of an impact that can have on your portfolio). That's the price you pay to invest, right? Wrong!

After a bit of research, I noted that the inexpensive index funds at Vanguard charged fees closer to .3%. With a bit of ingenuity, I could get those fees down to .1%. That was PER YEAR. All of the sudden, I was keeping most of my profits. I had eliminated most of the people in between my investments and me. My money started to grow!

Here are the facts: Costs are directly correlated with your return on investment. High costs will reduce your returns. Low costs will increase your returns. Your goal should be to cut those costs as much as possible so you can increase your yearly return year after year and decade after decade.

Your money will compound at a much greater rate after you get rid of all of the people between you and your investments. You can do this by owning only no-load index mutual funds. It worked for me and it can work for you. Believe it!

"Invest in low-turnover, passively managed index funds, and stay away from profit-driven investment management organizations. The mutual fund industry is a colossal failure resulting from its systematic exploitation of individual investors as funds extract enormous sums from investors in exchange for providing a shocking disservice. Excessive management fees take their toll, and manager profits dominate fiduciary responsibility."

- **David Swensen,** Chief Investment Officer of Yale University

28

A B C

Do you pay a load when you invest in mutual funds? If that question didn't make any sense to you, you probably do. A load is a four-letter word that your mom should have warned you about, but probably didn't know herself. It's a commission. It's a way for the financial industry "helpers" to skim off your investment returns either at the beginning, in the rear, or on a yearly basis.

For those of you who are unfamiliar with that first paragraph, I challenge you to go find your last statement and see if you have any of those letters (A, B, or C) attached to the mutual funds you may own. Yes, I would like you to put this book/tablet/computer/phone/device down and start digging. Go ahead. I will wait patiently.

What did you find out? Here is what we know. (1) Class A loads will slice off a chunk of money right when you invest with a "helper." That load costs you 5.75% for most stock mutual funds and about 4% for most bond mutual funds. (2) Class B loads will take the money out when you exit the fund. (3) Class C loads take the money out each and every year. It's kind of like running a marathon with a very large 50-pound weight attached to your neck. The results will not meet your expectations.

Here is an example: You give your local fee-based advisor $5,000 to invest. He sticks that money in a Class A load managed fund that runs you about 1% a year. You are automatically out $287.50 ($5,000 – 5.75%). This leaves you with $4,712.50 that will be invested in that expensive managed fund. You will have to earn 6.11% for the year just to break even based on the load and then you will have to make another 1% to break even on the high fee managed mutual fund. Informed investors do not play this game.

When I started investing, I paid a load. Why? I didn't know any better. Years later, I learned that I didn't have to pay a load. I could invest directly with an investment company and bypass the "helper." That was the last time I paid a load. This should be the last time YOU pay a load.

The majority of people who invest money into mutual funds pay a load. Why? They don't know what they don't know. The load means absolutely nothing in relation to the investment you are making. Actually, that's not quite true. A load locks in managed mutual funds with high yearly fees that YOU will pay year after year as long as you own that fund. That's not wise.

How do you avoid that? First, avoid the "helpers." Paying them a load so you can get a lower return on your money makes no sense at all. Take your money and go directly to the investment company that holds those mutual funds. My recommended option is Vanguard.

As stated earlier, I have no relationship with Vanguard. They do not pay me to recommend their company. Actually, I recommend you avoid most of what Vanguard offers. Avoid individual stocks, managed mutual funds, ETFs, and any other option that does not have the word "index" attached to it. (The Target Retirement and Lifestrategy funds would be the exception. They own an assortment of Vanguard index mutual funds, which could serve you quite well over long stretches of time.)

As time went on, I gravitated to index funds. I recommend you do the same. Thanks to one amazing man, John Bogle, you can invest at a minimal cost with those inexpensive no-load index mutual funds so you end up keeping most of your return on investment. It's a no-brainer.

"An investor doesn't have a prayer of picking a manager that can deliver true alpha."

- **Eugene Fama**, Nobel Laureate in Economics

29

SURVIVORSHIP BIAS

This type of bias can, and in many cases does provide performance numbers that don't reflect reality. It is very important to understand this point. In the financial industry, when a mutual fund dies (poor performance is usually the culprit), their performance dies with them. What does that mean? It's like a human being who died and every trace of their life was wiped out as if he or she did not exist.

The vast majority of mutual fund data does not include the records of the dead actively managed mutual funds (this is called survivorship bias). If the dead funds were counted, actively managed funds would fare much worse than they already do compared to index funds. Not counting the dead funds skews the results in a way that makes active management look better than it really is. Now let's dig a bit deeper.

There are many mutual funds that die every year due to poor performance. The industry is always trying new techniques and new management as they try to drum up business for the next "great" thing or maybe the next great "man." This is when the word *incubator* enters our vocabulary. Many mutual fund companies incubate funds (funds that are not open to the public) in a way that defines the winners and the losers.

Here is an example: Mutual Fund A does really well compared to its benchmark index for the past year with a return of 15%. Mutual Fund B does poorly compared to its benchmark index with a return of -2%. The mutual fund company keeps Mutual Fund A and promotes its great performance to the public. Mutual Fund B is put to rest and that -2% is put to rest with it (the results are buried and never make it into the historical return data). This demonstrates how the industry hides the facts.

When a mutual fund company brags about how many funds have beaten the index over a certain time period, it's a deception at best, and an outright lie at worst. They are not counting the dead mutual funds and their poor performance.

Why do they do it? These companies know that the regular investor is overly influenced by past performance numbers. They know that money flows in when they promote a four or five star fund (top quartiles in the category) and money flows out when there are one and two star funds. Let me state the obvious. Money flowing in is better for business than money flowing out.

So now what? When you see marketing that promotes a certain mutual fund company and their performance in relation to index funds, be skeptical. You now have a better understanding of what is going on behind the scenes. You are seeing how the cook makes the meal and it's not so pretty when that cook works in the financial services industry!

The bottom line is true today as it has been over the past four decades. Index funds that track large broadly diversified markets owning stocks and bonds all over the world consistently beat actively managed funds. That is the truth that the industry would prefer you not know.

Whether you are comparing small companies, large companies, U.S. stocks, international stocks, corporate bonds, government bonds, or any other investment that provides an index option, you are wise to buy the index and pay the lower cost. The odds are in your favor and they increase the longer you own those index funds. Survive with index funds!

"Unless an investor has access to 'incredibly high-qualified professionals,' they should be 100 percent passive -- that includes almost all individual investors and most institutional investors."

- **David Swensen**, Chief Investment Officer at Yale University

30

RISK WITHOUT REWARD

There are certain types of asset classes that provide you with plenty of risk without the proper amount of reward. It is important to identify these investments and avoid them. It may take more than one reading of this chapter to fully comprehend this very important issue.

Here are three asset class categories I recommend you avoid or limit in your portfolio: Small-cap growth companies, long-term bonds, and high-yield bonds (junk bonds). Why? You are not rewarded with the right amount of high returns in relation to the high risks you are taking. This is not just my personal opinion on the matter. Research based on past historical returns identifies this argument to be true.

(1) **Small-cap growth stock** gets a lot of attention. These securities tend to get analyzed to death and that causes many of them to be traded often as their price goes up, up and away. When reality hits, they fall hard and their historical return in relation to their risk is poor.

Do not own more small growth companies than you have to (you will own these stocks in a total stock market index fund and that is just fine, just don't own more). High risk and moderate return should be shunned and eliminated from consideration.

(2) **Long-term bonds** (long maturities) provide slightly higher returns on your money than intermediate-term bonds (shorter maturities), but their risk is much higher based on the effect of rising interest rates (when rates go up bonds get clobbered). Again, you are not properly compensated based on the risk you are assuming. Avoid owning long-term bonds. Stick with short-term and intermediate-term bonds.

(3) **High-yield bonds** (bonds that are issued by companies and municipalities that are rather sickly, which is why they are called junk bonds) should be avoided as well. They do provide higher returns than highly rated bonds (bonds issued by companies and municipalities that have strong financials), but you also incur much higher risk as some of the bonds will not pay out (especially when the economy goes into recession). Stay away from the junk!

Some people will disagree with me on these three asset classes and whether you should own them. Those people see the value of adding these asset classes to a portfolio based on the diversification issue. I get that, but I don't believe you need to invest in risky assets that don't pay you back fairly for the risk you are taking. You want a risk-adjusted return that makes investing in an asset category worth it. These three don't make the cut.

Here is a brief recap: When taking risk, stick with stocks rather than bonds (own bonds for their income and stability when stocks are headed down). When considering the length of maturities for bonds, stick with maturities under 10 years. Finally, avoid the junk. The return is not worth the risk you are taking on debt that comes with a great deal of risk.

Here is the bottom line: Only take risk when you are properly compensated for it. Respond accordingly with your portfolio allocations and you should end up with lower risk that provides higher returns over time on your money.

"High-powered, professional salespeople often tempt investors to buy products that offer seemingly attractive benefits. Unfortunately, the benefits are often either illusory or are accompanied by costs that far exceed these benefits."

- **Larry Swedroe,** *The Only Guide to Alternative Investments You'll Ever Need*

31

TIMING THE MARKET

Do you think you can time the market? You know, pick the right time to buy and sell different securities. Can you do it with individual stocks? What about ETFs or mutual funds?

Do you believe that you are a bit smarter than the next guy or gal when investing your money in the stock or bond markets? Do you think you can get in and get out just in time to avoid the big drops, while still catching the big ups that the markets can provide?

Did you say yes to any of those questions? I hope you didn't. The informed investor answers with a very quick NO to all of those questions when he or she is presented with them. Timing the market is a loser's game. The successful investor knows this and refuses to get pulled into this kind of manic behavior that produces low returns and high taxes and costs.

It's important that you learn to avoid this idea of timing the market. Your money and your future may depend upon it in some very big ways. Here is the truth. It is a fool's errand to try to time the market. The research tells us this simple fact. Collectively, investors do terribly when trying to time the market. Yet, human beings continue try. Why?

Here are three pretty good reasons. (1) Our brain is hard-wired to see order in a disorderly world. (2) We are inundated by people on television, magazines, and elsewhere who promote the idea of timing the market as they attempt to predict the future. (3) It is fun, exciting, exhilarating, and maybe even a bit of an ego boost as you try to outsmart others in this challenge of wits.

There are more reasons than those three, but they are a good start. Let's go ahead and state the obvious. Many people sabotage themselves and their investments needlessly. It's dangerous, it shouldn't be done, and very few people do it well in any given time period. When someone does pull it off, we call that person a genius. They aren't. They just got lucky in the vast majority of cases.

How can you avoid these mistakes? Become mindful of the human condition and the mistakes you can make. Read Jason Zweig's wonderful book, *Your Money & Your Brain*. Zweig's book provides many answers to why humans do what they do AND what you can do to avoid those life altering mistakes. Know thyself.

This is all part of the transformation, as you become the wise and informed investor. In the final analysis, it comes down to you and how much you are willing to educate yourself on the matter. The empirical data continues to point to the poor results of market timing. Market timing has no place in the life of the successful investor.

The informed investor comes to that realization. I did after years of delusional thinking that I could beat the markets. So did John Bogle and Charles Ellis and Burton Malkiel and Rick Ferri and Daniel Solin and Larry Swedroe and Frank Armstrong and Jack Meyer and Daniel Kauneman and William Bernstein and Eugene Fama and Paul Samuelson and William Sharpe and Merton Miller and...

"If there are 10,000 people looking at the stocks and trying to pick winners, 1 in 10,000 is going to score, by chance alone, a great coup, and that's all that's going on. It's a game, it's a chance operation, and people think they are doing something purposeful...but they're really not."

- **Merton Miller**, Nobel Laureate in Economics

32

THE CROOKS

When investing your money, you must avoid the crooks who will attempt to swindle away most, if not all, of what you have accumulated in your lifetime. That sounds pretty simple, right? Here's the problem. Crooks in the financial industry don't look like crooks walking the streets. In many cases, crooks in the financial industry look very professional with their suits, cars, homes, and credentials. They are hard to spot, but they are there, I can promise you that.

You do know who Bernie Madoff is, right? How about the Enron boys? How about the Wolf of Wall Street? There are many others, but let's take a look at these three cases from the recent past as we highlight the types of crooks you must avoid. Millions of dollars were swindled and ultimately lost because of these crooks and yet, while it was happening, people were singing their praises. What gives?

Let's start with Bernie Madoff. Bernie was a hedge fund manager who promised guaranteed returns of 10% or more to his wealthy and famous clients whether the markets were going up or down. That should have been a red flag, but as long as people got their money, they didn't seem to care. They should have.

Bernie ran a Ponzi scheme. There was no real investing going on. He took new investors money and paid the old investors with it. As with any Ponzi scheme, it worked as long as there was new money coming in. When the new money dried up, the house of cards fell and many, many people lost their life savings. What is the moral of the story? NO ONE can promise guaranteed returns at 10% or more. NO ONE! If they do, they are a crook or delusional. In either case, you need to run away!

Enron became one of the largest companies in the world, but only because the crooks ran two sets of books, one for the IRS and the other for a select few who were clued in on the scheme. Many employees got caught up in the rising stock price and sold their diversified mutual funds while putting their whole retirement in Enron stock. The company collapsed, the crooks went to jail or died, and the employees lost their jobs and their retirement money. It was and still is a very sad tale.

NEVER put your retirement money in one stock. I will go one step farther. As soon as you can, sell all individual stocks in your retirement plan and buy broadly diversified index mutual funds that own thousands of individual stocks and bonds. NEVER forget Enron and the damage those crooks caused.

The Wolf of Wall Street is a true story about a con artist who figured out how to make a fortune on Wall Street by selling penny stocks to uninformed investors looking for a big return. Jordan Belfort ended up going to prison, but he ruined many lives before the authorities caught up to him and his scheme.

Belfort was a good talker and a great salesman. Those qualities can be disastrous for investors if they belong to a crook like Jordan Belfort. Many people got sucked in based on Belfort's personality and skills as a slick-talking "expert." When someone is selling you riches over the phone, a red flag should go up. Hang up the phone!

There are crooks out there today wheeling and dealing. They are smart, they are slick, and in many cases, they look like upstanding citizens. Watch yourself AND your money!

"I've studied pathological liars, and anything they say, they believe, and that's one of the reasons they're so convincing, because they have no connection with the truth. It's a dead issue. It's like they're color-blind to the truth. So anything that comes out of their mouths is their reality."

- **Jane Velez-Mitchell**

33

THE BUBBLES

Bubbles in the investment markets have taken away fortunes and ruined lives going back a very long way. If you don't take the time to learn about the history of markets and the bubbles that followed, you are prone to repeating those events. Allow me to state the obvious. You will pay a severe price if you stay ignorant on the subject of bubbles.

Here are two wonderful books that will enlighten you on past bubbles in markets all over the world: *A Random Walk Down Wall Street*, by Burton Malkiel and *The Four Pillars of Investing*, by William Bernstein. Here is a primer that should help you better understand the situation prior to reading those informative books.

Anything that is traded or purchased on an open market can find itself in a bubble. We could be talking about stocks, bonds, commodities (gold and silver, for example), real estate and even tulips (see my book, *Financial Happine$$* to learn about the tulip bubble). Humans go too far on the up side and the down side in just about everything they do when they get excited or fearful about whatever it is being hyped at that moment.

The dot-com bubble and the fairly recent housing bubble are two very good cases. In both instances, securities and homes were purchased at ridiculous prices because they were expected to keep going up in the immediate future. This is called speculation.

You buy something not because of its real value, but because you believe some other sucker will pay more for it in the future. This is how bubbles start, continue, and ultimately collapse.

The dot-com bubble began innocently enough with excitement about the Internet and the many new businesses that were being launched to take advantage of this new and exciting world. But it got out of hand as all bubbles do. Pretty soon everyone was talking about these dot-com companies and their projections (speculative predictions about the future earnings of these companies).

The technology market went crazy and pretty soon people had their neighbors, friends, and family talking about how well their investments were doing thanks to those awesome dot-com companies. This caused others to jump on board so they did not miss out on the big payday. Hysteria followed and so did a market collapse. It got real ugly.

The housing bubble in the early part of the 21st century did not end any better. You had brokers and companies pushing no documentation loans (called "liar loans" by some folks) as they pushed people into homes they could not afford, but in the end, it was regular human beings who signed on the dotted line. There was plenty of fault to go around (politicians included). Housing prices skyrocketed and then collapsed as many homes fell into foreclosure. Many people walked away with nothing.

So how do you avoid these bubbles? First, it is harder than it sounds. Many people think they can get in and get out of bubbles. Don't buy into that way of thinking. Study your history. Study human psychology. Study herd behavior. Bubbles ruin lives. Don't let it happen to you.

"Be aware that the markets make regular trips to the loony bin in both directions. There will be times when new technologies promise to remake our economy and culture and that by getting in on the ground floor, you will profit greatly. When this happens, hold on tight to your wallet. There will also be times when the sky seems to be falling. These are usually good times to buy."

- **William Bernstein**, *The Four Pillars of Investing*

34

THE BREAK ROOM

The break room is a very dangerous place to be for the uninformed and ill-prepared investor. This is the place where your co-workers hang out and share stories and sage advice on all kinds of topics. One of those subjects may just be the world of investing. Look out! What they are sharing, you don't want in most cases.

The break room it is a very hazardous place to be learning about investing your money. It might be Bill who is talking about his gold investments, Martha who brags about her "safe" annuity, or maybe Clint who tells you how to sell the mutual funds in your 401(k) so you can buy the company's individual stock. These types of people can make the break room a very treacherous place if you're not careful.

The break room is full of all kinds of "experts" and they are generally quick to share their "expertise" with anyone who will listen to them. In almost all cases, these people are not experts and they hold no expertise in the world of investing. They spin stories, some are anecdotal, some are fabrications, some involve people reciting what others have said to them, and some are just plain ignorant.

I am not saying your co-workers are bad people. I am not even saying they are trying to do you harm. I am saying they can sway you toward believing in the things they believe in and that is dangerous. Sometimes these folks are the old guard at work. Sometimes they are the new managers who just landed there out of college. Sometimes they may run in packs, gobbling up unsuspecting workers throughout the day. Don't let them gobble you up!

How can you protect yourself from these so-called "experts?" Read the books written by the authors I have highlighted. These individuals are the true experts when you are ready to learn about investing. Learning from the real experts will provide you with the protection you will need when you step into the very hazardous break room.

Protection? I see this education you are receiving as a protective bubble. A bubble that takes that crap you hear in the break room and stops it from reaching your mind and ultimately your behaviors. It bounces off and does not stick!

Thanks to those true experts and the books they write, you have access to the truth when it comes to investing. You are not stuck listening to a small group of people in your physical world. You have access to some great minds outside of your physical world.

I have never met John Bogle, William Bernstein, Charles Ellis, Daniel Solin, Jason Zweig, Larry Swedroe, Frank Armstrong, Rick Ferri, Charles Ellis, David Swensen or Burton Malkiel, but they have helped me a great deal in my life.

These wise men enter my world whenever I pick up their books and read their words. They become my teammates going forward in this scary investing world as I take action with what I have learned. They can do the same for you. Join our team!

"A nationwide survey of 750 investors found that 74% expected that their mutual funds would "consistently beat the S&P 500 every year" —even though most funds fail to outperform the Standard & Poor's 500 stock index in the long run, and many funds fail to beat it in any given year."

- **Jason Zweig**, *Your Money & Your Brain*

35

THE HERD

Do you follow the herd? Many people do, especially when it comes to investing. If you ask them why they invest their money with this "helper" or at that place, they tend to mention others who also do it. Investing based on what others are doing will not serve you well in many cases. Running with the herd is a mistake much of the time.

So why do people run with the herd? Actually, I don't think this is very hard to understand. When you are doing what others are doing, it can make you feel safe and secure. When you are on your own, it can be a bit scary. Running with the herd makes us feel better, but at what cost?

Let's take a moment and define the herd as I see it in the year 2015. Many individuals have no idea what they are invested in. Basically, they are winging it, as they trust "their guy." Is that you? Are you part of that herd? Here is one way to tell. Describe right now what investments you have and what each one is costing you per year in loads and fees. If you cannot do that, you are very likely part of the herd.

Why is being part of the herd so dangerous? You don't have a clue about what is going on with your investments for one thing. When you hear the market is dropping fast, it scares the hell out of you even if you don't know what markets you are invested in. That lack of knowledge keeps you running with the herd. Danger! Danger! Danger!

Let's just lay it out nice and clear. You don't want to be part of the herd. The herd is running, but they don't know where they are heading. Many people get trampled when they get caught up with the herd. It can cost you a great deal of money, time and energy. Reject the herd!

So how does a person avoid being part of the herd? Start reading from the independent sources I continue to reference (it is not an accident that you are getting some repetitive messages). You will see a long list of books in the back of this book that will move you in the right direction on the topic. Whether you are a beginner, intermediate, or advanced person on the subject, it's time to separate yourself from the herd.

Take some time and understand *confirmation bias*. This particular bias causes us to seek out information that confirms our current beliefs, while discounting information that runs counter to what we believe in. DO NOT let confirmation bias stop you from learning new information.

As you become more knowledgeable on the subject, you will "see" what the informed investor sees and that will cause you to distance yourself from most of the financial industry. Seek out those independent voices that will guide you down the right path. Here are two books that can help the beginning investor.

- *The Little Book of Common Sense Investing* by John Bogle.

- *The Smartest Investment Book You'll Ever Read* by Daniel Solin.

Move away from the herd!

"The overwhelming number of mutual-fund investors clearly suffer at the hands of the mutual-fund industry. Some of the causes—outrageous fees, excessive trading, and bloated assets-stand as obvious culprits in producing performance deficits. Other factors—unethical kickbacks and indefensible distribution practices—remain generally hidden from view. An examination of the sources of mutual-fund industry's performance deficit serves to buttress the argument in favor of passive management."

- **David Swensen,** *Unconventional Success*

36

REVERSION TO THE MEAN

What goes up, will come down at some point. What goes down; will go up eventually. That is a rough definition of *reversion to the mean* (also referred to as regression to the mean). This concept tends to hang out with his good buddy, *recency bias*. They both set up the average investor for a pretty hard fall based on the ups and downs of the markets. Education on the matter can reduce that pain. Let's take a look.

It is of critical importance that the average investor becomes aware of the average returns garnered by the stock and bond markets over the past 90 years or so. No, I am not saying those returns tell us what the future returns will be, but they do give us a glimpse of what we can expect and what seems unlikely to happen. Let's take a look at an example.

You have selected an asset allocation of 60% stocks and 40% bonds. Your return last year after costs was 16% and the previous year's return was 18%. Is that normal? No. The average annual return for that allocation mix over the last 88 years before costs was 8.9%. That number is well below those two years where you made 16% and 18%.

So what are we to take from that? The next year or so could find our yearly return far below 8.9% as the markets revert back to their historical averages based on our asset allocation of stocks and bonds. Do we know exactly when that will happen? No, not at all, but we do know that markets revert to the mean over time and we should not be surprised when that occurs. And yet many people are astounded. You see, many people jump on the bandwagon only after they see big results. That is a really bad idea. They are chasing performance.

People chase performance all of the time. They wait until some type of investment has gone up and then they "throw their hat into the ring." What happens? Markets revert to the mean, and those same investors get jerked around by receiving returns far below historical market averages. Then, the investor gets out of the market and within short order the market mean reverts again, going back up. This is the life of far too many investors throughout the world. Don't be one of them!

How do you avoid this manic behavior? The simple answer is don't chase performance. Don't wait for markets to go down or up before investing your money. Get in the game and stay in the game for as long as possible while ignoring the day-to-day gyrations that occur.

Identify your desired asset allocation numbers (how much you want in stocks vs. how much you want in bonds and cash), buy the stock and bond funds using no-load index mutual funds, and then rebalance them over time within retirement accounts or by dollar-cost averaging the money into your investments (having a selected amount automatically invested over a specific time period).

There is no timing the market. There is no picking the right market or the right sector. There is no listening to this guru or that guru telling you what to do, where to be, and how much to put there. This idea of strategic asset allocation is sound (buy and hold investments over all parts of the world). It has proven itself in very positive ways over many decades. It reduces your costs and taxes (and stress), which ultimately provides you higher returns over time.

"After costs, only the top 3% of managers produce a return that indicates they have sufficient skill to just cover their costs, which means that going forward, and despite extraordinary past returns, even the top performers are expected to be only as good as a low-cost passive index fund. The other 97% can be expected to do worse."

- **Eugene Fama**, Nobel Laureate in Economics

37

UNCLE JOE

Anyone have a relative who is always bragging about his stock picking abilities? You know, he tells you how he made a killing on Apple, Facebook, Twitter, Alibaba, or whatever is the hot stock or IPO at the time. I call this person Uncle Joe.

This person sticks his chest out and makes you think he is a wizard when it comes to investing money as he picks the winners and avoids the losers. He is not the wizard he thinks he is, and I need you to know that as early in life as possible.

It doesn't have to be Uncle Joe. It could be Aunt Louise, cousin Jim, sister Susan, or even close friend Bill. The names change, but the behavior doesn't. You have a person who talks about their apparent success in the stock market as they ignore other very important factors that should not be left out of the mix like commissions, loads, fees, and taxes.

Here is a little secret just between you and me. Uncle Joe is very likely a blowhard who likes to brag about the times he got lucky in picking some type of investment. Luck does not equal skill. He may not know it, but you need to. Uncle Joe has a tendency to fabricate what he has done to make himself sound smart and wise when it comes to investing. He is selective in what he talks about and what he doesn't.

Uncle Joe brags about his winners, but he fails to mention his losers. Kind of like the guy who goes to Vegas and tells you how he hit a jackpot on the slots. He doesn't tell you how much money he lost elsewhere! We must account for the entire picture when evaluating how we have done with our investments.

I seriously doubt Uncle Joe has a clue about how his portfolio has done after costs (commissions, loads, and fees) and taxes. Ignoring these costs and the losing investments doesn't make them go away. Allow me to state the obvious. Uncle Joe is someone that should be ignored and exposed for what he is. An uninformed investor who talks a good game but really has no idea about how the investing game works.

That probably sounded a little rough, but this is serious business, and I think it is important to identify ignorance when you hear it and see it. Uncle Joe spends way too much time trading individual stocks and other types of securities and too little time educating himself on the business of investing by reading the books from the true experts in the field.

The wise investors spend most of their time educating themselves on the subject and a small amount of time buying and selling their investments. The informed investors know that buying and selling often is a really bad idea and should be avoided all along the way.

Here is a bonus. If you know an "Uncle Joe," ask him what his AFTER cost return was over the last 1, 3, 5, and 10 year time periods. I am betting there will be silence when you pose the question. Here are my returns after costs as of January 9, 2015. The informed and successful investor will know the after cost return on their investment. Be that person!

- 1 Year return: **7.8%**
- 3 year average: **13.5%**
- 5 year average: **11.4%**
- 10 year average: **9.1%** (includes the miserable 2008 market returns)

"Market timing, like stock picking is nothing but a shell game. You should never listen to anyone who says he or she can time the market, no matter how qualified or confident that person appears to be."

- **Daniel Solin,** *The Smartest Investment Book You'll Ever Read*

38

FAMILY

How did the family make it into an investment book? Family plays a pretty important role in most people's lives. In many cases, the advice your family gives you is well meaning as they try to help you to avoid the pitfalls of life. Help? They tell you what to do! Does that sound familiar to anyone?

Here is a question. What happens when family members provide you bad information or bad direction? It happens and it probably occurs much more often than any of us would like to believe.

It makes sense that we should listen to the older generation as they pass on wisdom to the younger generation. This could include the topic of investing. Here is where I see a problem. Do mom and dad understand the world of investing? What about Uncle Joe? What advice do they provide that will help you become a wise and successful investor? Let's take a look at a couple of possible scenarios.

Let's start with Dad. He could very well be providing information passed on to him from his dad, but did grandpa know what he was talking about when it came to investing? Dad could also be passing on "knowledge" based on what he heard in the break room at work. Is that the kind of wisdom you are going to use to invest your money?

Now let's take a look at Mom. Here is what we know about a lot of mothers. They want you to be safe and secure. They don't want you to get hurt or suffer. They don't want you to take on any unneeded risks that would cause you harm. Does that sound familiar? Mom is going to be risk averse in many cases. Fear could cause her to push you to "play it safe" with your investments AND your life. Hmmm...

How about Uncle Joe? We have covered him already, but he also can play a very important role in this process. If he "guides" you on what to invest in, do you follow his advice? At some point, do you just throw up your arms and give in and do what he says? It happens for many folks, but you should not let that happen to you.

You should not pick up your investing education from your family! Ouch. I know that statement probably offended some of you, but it's true in the vast majority of cases. Yes, if your dad is Warren Buffett or John Bogle, you should listen carefully to their advice, but let's face it, those men are not part of most families.

The truth is, most family members don't know what they are talking about when it comes to investing. That does not make them bad people. It doesn't make them stupid either. It simply identifies how little so many people know about the world of investing, which is why we need to continue to seek out those true independent experts. Stay very skeptical about what you hear at home!

Let's wrap this up with a brief summary. Your family loves you or least I hope they do. They look out for you and try to help you when you ask for help (and in many cases when you don't). Just be careful with all that "wisdom" they are providing. Nod your head, smile when advice is given, and then go to the true experts to confirm or refute what you are hearing at home. YOU must go get the answers you seek.

"Most investors, both institutional and individual, will find the best way to own common stocks is through an index fund that charges minimal fees. Those following this path are sure to beat the net results (after fees and expenses) delivered by the great majority of investment professionals."

- **Warren Buffett**

39

CHASING STARS

Do you chase stars? Here I am talking about chasing after 4- and 5-star mutual funds. When looking to invest your money, do you eliminate all of your options except the very best past performing funds with the highest returns? If you do, this is called *chasing performance*. (I know this subject has been mentioned already, but more depth on the matter is needed.)

Let's take a step back and review the situation. You are ready to start investing. You look at your options and see mutual funds that have done very well in the past. They receive 4 or 5 stars (5 being the highest a fund can receive) from a mutual fund tracking agency like Morningstar. You say to yourself, "I want the best," so you pick the ones that have performed the best in the past. That may make sense in your brain, but it's a mistake in real life.

Past performance does not predict future results. The amount of stars a mutual fund has is irrelevant when considering which fund to select. Ignore them and the companies and people who push them. Stick with those no-load index funds that I keep referencing. This will provide you access to low-fee investments. Fees do matter and they do correlate to higher returns over time. Focus on fees, not stars.

Let's review how chasing stars works (for them, not you). You become informed on the subject and invest in nothing but index funds. Some "helper" sends you information that shows how a particular managed mutual fund beat its index. If you had owned this fund, you would have come out ahead in relation to the benchmark indexes. He is not lying to you, but he is also not telling you the whole story, which is why it pays to be educated on this bit of trickery.

When someone identifies a few managed mutual funds that beat an index, they are withholding how many did not. They are showing you one of the 20% or so mutual funds that outperformed their benchmark indexes. They are not showing you the 80% of mutual funds that failed to beat those indexes (don't forget about the dead ones). The investment company has turned into a marketing company and that is very dangerous for YOU.

They pull you in by giving you a small bit of information. They advertise the more expensive managed funds with 4- and 5- star ratings (sometimes with a load that is not reflected on the returns) that beat the indexes as they attempt to get you to switch. You have to learn to see through this kind of marketing approach.

We all want to own the best investments, but buying past performance won't allow you to do that. It is critically important to remind yourself of that very important fact. Chasing performance is one of the worst things you can do as an investor. Far too many investors jump on high-flying mutual funds only to see poor results going forward. Then they jump off and go after the next high-flying mutual fund only to see that investment drop in value. Don't be that person.

So what are you to do about this deceitful game played by many investment companies and their "helpers?" That's easy. Keep educating yourself so you won't fall for this dishonest approach. The right education served up by the right teachers will set you free.

"Morningstar's vaunted five-star rating system rests on the precarious foundation of historical performance numbers. Yet the assignment of a four-star or five-star rating to a mutual fund carries enormous influence on flows of investor funds. Just as in The Wizard of Oz, a pathetic little man stands behind the curtain. Chasing performance produces disastrous results for investors."

- **David Swensen,** *Unconventional Success*

Shooting Stars

The chart provides data taken from the mutual fund tracking agency, Morningstar. This illustration shows how the top 10 mutual funds performed since the year 2000.

Going from number 1 to number 2,042 happens more times than you might imagine. Similar time periods show similar results. The message should be clear, do not chase the stars!

Mutual Fund	2000	2001	2002	2003	2004
Evergreen Health Care	1	2,042	3,952	493	3,241
Manning % Napier Life	2	309	3,153	2,236	4,747
Munder Health	3	4,013	4,743	459	2,076
BlackRock Global	4	2,459	1,371	185	8
Allianz RCM Biotech	5	4,225	4,785	962	1,366
Eaton Vance World	6	2,810	4,219	2,503	3,549
Icon Energy	7	2,512	1,906	1,750	32
JennDry Jenn Health	8	2,333	4,605	810	154
Allianz RCM	9	3,544	4,267	2,319	1,995
Fidelity Select	10	4,116	2,178	2,351	22

40

RECENCY BIAS

Human beings are interesting creatures. We tend to see something occur and then expect it to repeat itself again, and again, and again. We are overly influenced by the recent past as we look toward the future. In the world of investing, this is called *recency bias*. It sounds innocent enough, but this is a very dangerous thing. It is critical that you learn about it and see it when it pops up in every day life.

A story that relates to real life is probably the best way to explain this concept. Let's take a look at the housing bubble that took place in the recent past. I have selected this one example of recency bias because it is still fresh in many people's minds. Mind you, I had many options to pick from that took place long before this most recent collapse. Feel free to Google "bubbles" and "recency bias" to see many more examples.

All around America, the prices of homes were going up, up and away soon after we entered the year 2000. Many of us had friends and family bragging about how much their homes had gone up in price. They were going to make a fortune as they sold their old home, bought a new one, and then kept doing it until they were worth millions! That's not how it works, but on occasion markets go crazy. Disaster would soon strike.

These homeowners were caught up in the moment and that is very human. The most recent past had homes going up by 10% or more per year. This was not sustainable. The historical return on real estate runs parallel with inflation and that puts it at something close to 3.5% per year over the last 90 years or so. But your home went up 12% two years ago, and 14% last year. Next year it is sure to go up 16%, right? I am afraid that is not correct and the people who thought that, paid a severe penalty.

That is how recency bias works. People disregard (or don't even know) the historical returns on a particular investment whether that is real estate, bonds, stocks, gold, whatever, as they change their way of thinking based on the very recent past. Without knowing what is normal, we see the current trend as normal. This is dangerous!

This is also how bubbles start to take shape. More and more people believe we are in a new time and the old rules don't apply. The old farts don't know what they are talking about when they warn us about the risks that come with this "new" type of thinking.

The world has changed, you say. This is a new day with new rules, you say. The problem is, you are defining the past as the last few years. The wise investor defines the past as the past few decades and even centuries. There is a big difference when we look at 90 years vs. 18 months.

It is very easy to see recent trends and patterns and somehow make them continue (in our mind) long into the future. Recency bias creates a future in our head that will not play out well in real life. By understanding that key point, you will be better prepared not only for what is currently happening, but also for what might happen in the not to far off future. Understand recency bias or pay a severe penalty.

"Back in December 1999, after five straight years in which the U.S. stock market had gained at least 20% investors expect to earn 18.4% on their stocks over the next twelve months. But by March 2003, after annual losses in 2000, 2001, and 2002, investors expected their stocks to go up 6.3% in the coming year. Their reliance on the recent past led investors to get the future exactly backwards: In 2000, rather than going up 18.4%, stocks dropped a shocking 9%; in the twelve months following March 2003, the U.S. market rose not a tepid 6.3% but a whopping 35.1%."

- **Jason Zweig,** *Your Money & Your Brain*

41

THE GLITTER

Do you invest in gold and/or silver? Why? Please pause and take a few minutes before answering that question. Why do you invest in something that has barely stayed up with inflation over the last 90 years or so AND has produced no yearly income?

I believe most people do not invest in gold or silver because of their historical return on investment. I don't think most people even know what those historical numbers are. I think most people invest in these two items because of fear and possibly greed. As stated earlier, allowing those emotions to creep into your investment decision-making can be hazardous to your wealth creating abilities. Let's take a look.

These two metals have some type of real hold on many people. You can touch them. You can store them in a safe place. They make people feel safe "just in case." Just in case? The talk of Armageddon seems to pop up, especially when the economy is in the crapper or some big nasty event takes place. People rush to these metals for safety and security. I get that people feel scared at times, but it's a mistake to buy the glitter when that happens.

Is it possible that Armageddon will happen? Sure. Is it probable? No. It's possible you will get hit by lightning, but not probable. Play the probabilities, not the possibilities. Keep this distinction in mind the next time someone screams about how the world is going to come to an end.

It is highly unlikely you or I will ever see the world come to an end and if it does, that hunk of metal is not going to serve you well when people show up at your door with guns. Avoid that kind of worst-case thinking and that means avoiding gold and silver.

Only invest in things that produce yearly income. That is a good rule of thumb, which will help you avoid the majority of bad investments. Gold and silver are two of those bad investments. This would also stop you from investing in art, coins, timeshares, undeveloped land, and Uncle Joe's new invention. If it doesn't produce yearly dividends, interest, capital gains, rent, etc., stay away from it.

I know some of you will disregard this message. You may not agree with the points I am making (many people end up reciting what salespeople say when they buy these commodities). You may think I underestimate the probabilities. You may just think I am crazy (you could be right on that one). It's okay to disagree with me, but you might want to continue to read about the issue from others.

Educate yourself elsewhere to see what independent sources have to say on the topic. Just make sure you avoid the people who sell gold and silver. They are not independent sources. They are selling a product using fear or greed to scare you into buying something that benefits them much more than you. This includes celebrities who are paid big bucks to smile into the camera and tell you how gold or silver make them feel "safe."

Some people invest in these metals as a hedge against other investments. In theory, this can make some sense. In reality, I don't buy it. These metals don't belong in your investment portfolio. If you own them, sell them and buy index funds. If you don't own them, steer clear of the marketing campaigns that push them.

"Those who buy and sell commodities are not investing; they are speculating that they know more or better than the market knows. They may be right with their bets and trades, but for every right there must be an equal wrong. The total of all trading adds up to a negative—a zero-sum game minus the costs of trading."

- **Charles Ellis**, *Winning the Loser's Game*

42

The ETF

The exchange-traded fund (ETF) has captured the interest of many, many investors all over the world. These types of investments are used every day in America and elsewhere to own securities at a very low cost. They are almost identical to owning a very inexpensive, broadly diversified index fund. In theory, they are great. In actual application, they fail. I recommend you stay away from them.

Let's take a moment to explain what an ETF is. The exchange-traded fund looks a lot like an index fund. The good ones track broad indexes like the S&P 500, or maybe the Russell 3000 or Wilshire 5000. So far, so good I would say.

When you buy shares of an ETF, you are buying shares of a portfolio that tracks the yield and return of the index it is tracking. That sounds an awful lot like those index funds I like so much, so why do I not like ETFs? It's not the ETF that is the problem; it's how people use them.

Individuals trade them like individual stocks, and as we covered earlier, that is a really bad idea. Yes, you can now buy and sell ETFs commission-free in some instances, but many people violate a very big rule. They attempt to time the market by buying at a perfect time and then selling at a perfect time.

If individuals purchased a broadly diversified ETF that tracked a broad index like the S&P 500 and then held onto it for decades, I would say have at it, but that is rare. The majority of people trade ETFs just like individual stocks, which is why you should avoid them. Again, in theory they are good. In application they are not.

There are other problems as well. More and more ETFs are being created to "specialize" in certain sectors of the economy or certain parts of the world. This idea of trying to pick the right places to invest in will not serve you well. That is a game that the individual investor will lose as he/she buys and sells different ETFs throughout the year. Don't do it and don't let anyone talk you into doing it.

But ETFs are cheap! Yes, they are, but no-load stock and bond index fund Admiral Shares at vanguard.com are just as inexpensive. You can buy them with the same low expense ratios, and you can dollar cost average money into them each month (something you cannot do with an ETF), as you own them for decades.

Let's wrap this up and move on. There is nothing wrong with a broadly diversified ETF like the Spider, which tracks the S&P 500, if you buy it and own it for a couple of decades. That option would work just as effectively as an index fund that owns the same securities. The problems come into play when placing them in the hands of the average individual investor who becomes a trader rather than a long-term investor.

The average investor turns his/her ETFs into individual stocks as he/she trades them early and often. Timing the market and predicting future ups and downs is the natural behavior that follows. That is why you should stay away from the ETF (and brokers) and stick with those boring but very efficient no-load index mutual funds.

"I suspect that too many ETFs will prove, if not suicidal to their owners in financial terms, at least wealth-depleting. We know that ETFs are largely used by traders, for the turnover of Spider shares is running at a 3600 percent annual rate. The turnover for the NASDAQ Qubes is even higher, at 6,000 percent per year."

- **John Bogle**, *The Little Book of Common Sense Investing*

43

INVESTING IN YOUR HOME

What asset has been called the best and possibly only major investment that most people will make in their lifetime? The *personal home* is how many people answer that question. The informed investor knows the reality of the situation and why that statement should be discounted.

The personal home is not the great investment it is made out to be. Why? It comes down to costs. Far too many people focus on the before-cost return on their home instead of their after-cost return. That is a serious mistake you must avoid.

Here are the facts based on the historical research. Your personal home is going to track the yearly inflation rate very closely when you live in mid- to large-size cities. This means a return of about 3.5% (the ridiculous increases in appreciation in the first part of this century were an aberration and the massive collapse in prices signified that). After a period of 20 years, you could see a very nice increase in the value of your home. Let's take a look at an example.

- You buy a home in the year 2010 for **$200,000**

- After 20 years at 3.5% the value rises to **$397,957.77**

- That is a profit of **$197,957.77**

That is BEFORE you factor in the costs of homeownership. To see if it was a good investment, we must consider the AFTER costs return. What costs? Property taxes, insurance, interest on the loan, maintenance, and property upgrades. Those costs could easily reach **10% per year.**

Let's say the yearly tax reduction reduces that number by 2% per year (many people with relatively small mortgages will not see such a large benefit). That takes us to **8% per year** in costs. What does an 8% yearly cost run you on a $200,000 piece of property over 20 years?

$320,000!

You get an after cost return of **-$122,042.23** ($197,957.77 - $320,000). Yes, I know I am making a very simple illustration of a pretty complex situation, but do not disregard the point I am making. In most cases, you are going to lose money owning a personal home when you consider the costs. (I haven't even factored in the initial costs when buying or the closing costs, including a Realtor, when selling.)

Do not consider your home an investment. It is a consumption item that will cost you a great deal of money over time. Now I am not saying you shouldn't buy a home. If you have the 20% down payment saved up, and you can fit into the home relatively easily, go for it. Just stop looking at your home as some great investment. It's not.

While you're at it, stop listening to people who tell you that your personal home is a good investment. They are either uninformed or they work in the real estate industry (the real estate industry needs you to keep buying homes and selling homes to pay THEIR bills).

Your home will produce no yearly income (a good investment will produce yearly income in the form of dividends or rent for example). It may or may not stay up with inflation, and it will cost you a good portion of your monthly and yearly paycheck. Run the numbers and you will see that a personal home is a consumption item, not an investment.

"Homeownership is not an investment; it is exactly the opposite, a consumption item. After taking into consideration maintenance costs and taxes, you are often better off renting."

- **William Bernstein,** *The Investor's Manifesto*

44

ALTERNATIVES

This chapter may not make sense to some of you. It would not have made sense to me once upon a time. To others, it will hold some interest. Let's get into it. In the world of investing, there are alternative investments. What does "alternative" mean?

It usually means investments that are not transparent, expensive, and they tend to lock up your money for long periods of time without any real understanding about how they are performing. Interested? I hope not. Now let's take a look at how they are marketed in an attempt to garner your interest in plucking down your hard earned money.

Alternative investments (hedge funds, private equity, non-traded REITs, leveraged buyouts and funds, and covered calls are a short list that includes much more) are promoted to individual and institutional investors as a way to increase return outside the normal publicly-traded markets.

These are investments that are not usually offered to just anyone. You generally have to make a bunch of money or have a bunch of money to get invited into this very select group of investors.

Does that sound more exciting? I bet it did to some of you. We all like to feel special. We all like to think we are getting a better deal. That makes us human, but that does not make these types of investments good options. Bernie Madoff made his investors feel special. Hmmm…

The reality is, because you have a lot of money, you get the opportunity to take a lot more risk, pay a lot more in fees, while having the probability of getting lower returns. Congratulations?

Why do I even talk about these issues when most people won't have access to them? Because you do! You see, these investments are offered to high income/high net worth people AND large state pension systems (institutional investors) all over the United States. Guess whose money is being invested by those large institutions? Yep, it's money that is earmarked for the average person and their retirement.

Your state pension money is being thrown down this alternative world of investments, sometimes with disastrous results. Are you thinking that it's not your problem since you don't have a state pension? Guess who is on the hook in most cases if pensions go bust? The state taxpayer! Do I have your attention now?

If you are a high income/high net worth person you can decide for yourself if you want to get screwed by these investments. You can afford it and if you want to take large risks, while getting mediocre returns, that's your choice. As for the rest of us, we need to contact our elected officials and demand change with how our pension systems are being invested. You and I cannot afford the big risks that come with these types of investments.

The informed investor selects index funds (and they demand the same from the people who manage their pension money) as they reduce their risk, reduce their costs, and increase their returns over time. You can learn more by reading two wonderful books written by Larry Swedroe: *Chasing Alpha* and *The Only Guide to Alternative Investments You'll Ever Need.*

"Those institutions [state pension plans and endowments of state universities] are placing risky bets on private equity and similar funds, to some degree at the taxpayer's expense. They are relying on consultants who, on average, add no value and no prospect of delivering alpha. Taxpayers would be better served if public institutions adopted a low-cost index-based approach to endowment management."

- **Robert Huebscher**, 25+ years in the Financial Services Industry

45

HOW NOT TO DO IT

Here is a list of things you should not do when investing your money. This list could be bigger, but it will do for now. If any of these statements applies to you, it's time to change your ways. The future belongs to those who understand the landscape and how to find their way through the maze. Do not allow yourself to fall for these mistakes.

- Spend time with a stockbroker and listen to his/her advice.

- Invest in individual stocks based on a tip from a blog/website.

- Invest in individual stocks based on a television "expert."

- Invest in individual stocks based on intuition.

- Invest in penny stocks.

- Invest in IPOs.

- Go down to the local fee-based financial advisor for help.

- Invest in managed funds because your "guy" says so.

- Only invest in 4- and 5-star mutual funds.

- Go down to the local life insurance agent for help.

- Use life insurance to invest for your future.

- Invest in all kinds of annuities to get guaranteed returns.

- Do what "Uncle Joe" does. He is old and wise!

- Invest based off a newsletter from some "smart" guy.

- Invest in gold and silver.

- Invest in timeshares.

- Invest using calls, puts, options, futures, and margin.

- Invest in hedge funds and private equity.

- Invest in limited partnerships and private REITs.

- Try to get rich fast by picking winners and avoiding the losers.

There are more bad options than good options when investing your money. It is really important for you to know that. The financial services industry relies on your ignorance to promote and sell products and services that feed their retirement accounts, not yours. With a financial education, you can turn the tables.

"You don't need 99.9 percent of what Wall Street is selling. It's expensive, unsuitable, or stupid. Most investments are designed to profit the brokers, banks, and insurance companies, not you. They should carry a warning label: "Beware! This financial product may be injurious to your wealth!"

- **Jane Bryant Quinn**, Author of *Making the Most of Your Money*

Stage III

THE

PATH

FORWARD

46

RISK

How many people do you know who keep their money in the bank because it is "safe?" They avoid putting their money in the stock and/or bond markets because those markets are way too "risky." Sound familiar to anyone? That is dangerous thinking and the future value of one's money will suffer because of it.

Many people keep their money in the bank because it has no risk, or so they think. Here is the truth. There is risk in everything we do and that includes money in the bank. Yes, it might be safe from market risk (picture the ups and downs of the daily stock and bond markets), but don't let that cloud your judgment. You may never see the *dollar amount* of your money go down in the bank, but the *value* is going down thanks to that deadly thing called inflation. That big monster is taking a bite out of your money!

The money you keep in the bank is exposed to inflation risk. It is shrinking little by little right before your eyes. Here is an example. Let's say you are earning 1% on your "safe" savings account and inflation is running at 3.5%. That provides you a real return of -2.5% (real return = the nominal return minus the inflation rate). Your money is now worth less than it was a year ago and the compounded effect of that will be very big over a lifetime.

What is a person to do? One, accept the reality of inflation risk. Two, acknowledge there is no risk-free way to stash your money. Three, if your money is not growing, it is shrinking; it's that simple. That's why you should consider taking market risk with your money. You just do it wisely while only taking the amount of risk necessary to meet your goals and future needs. Now let's see how that can be done.

When you invest in the stock and bond markets you expose your money to market risk and you are guaranteed to see the value of your portfolio go down on occasion. Sometimes it will go down for a week, a month, or maybe even a year or more. That short-term risk is required if you want to grow your money over time. Risk is rewarded with higher returns, but that does not mean you should take unneeded risk.

This is why you should invest in no-load index mutual funds that diversify you all over the world in stocks and bonds. You end up owning thousands and thousands of individual stocks and bonds. When one is going down, another is going up. Sometimes they drop together. Sometimes they rise together. Over the long-term, the wise investor has been rewarded with returns far beyond the 3.5% inflation rate. You have been rewarded with about 10% per year for stocks and 5% for bonds.

Which stocks and which bonds should you own? All of them! There are a few nuances that we will cover later in the book, but the primary answer goes back to what John Bogle has been saying forever. "Don't look for the needle in the haystack, buy the haystack."

Mr. Bogle has been proven right time and again and the informed investor knows this. As you continue down this path toward becoming the wise and efficient investor, remind yourself, you take risk in the short-term so you can reap the rewards in the long-term.

"Fear stifles our thinking and actions. It creates indecisiveness that results in stagnation. I have known talented people who procrastinate indefinitely rather than risk failure. Lost opportunities cause erosion of confidence, and the downward spiral begins. Don't let the opinions of the average man sway you. Dream, and he thinks your crazy. Succeed, and he thinks your lucky. Acquire wealth, and he thinks your greedy. Pay no attention. He simply doesn't understand."

- **Charles Stanley**

47

STOCKS

Investing in stocks (also referred to as *equities*) scares a lot of people away. Why is that? I think we can narrow it down to three primary reasons.

(1) The individual fears losing the money they have worked so hard to save.
(2) The individual doesn't understand how investing in stocks works.
(3) The individual investor thinks investing in stocks is rigged.

Do any of those apply to you? All three of them applied to me at one point in my life, but they don't anymore. Why? I became educated on how the game is played and how I can make money playing that game. You can do the same. Let's take a look.

(1) I will lose all my money. In any given year stock markets can go down and sometimes by quite a bit. **You only lose money when you sell after the markets have dropped.** Just because you see the *value* of your portfolio go down, does not mean you have lost money. It just means the markets took a downward turn and your pot of money shrunk temporarily. That is no big deal and should be expected periodically. Remember, with risk, comes return. With return, comes risk.

(2) How does it work? Stocks are traded all over the world based on their perceived future value. **When you buy stocks, you are buying businesses that drive our economies**. Owning stocks equates to owning a small piece of those businesses. When you own a stock mutual fund, you end up owning hundreds, and possibly thousands, of businesses. This provides you the chance to share in their growth over time based on their earnings and paid out dividends. This has proven to be a very successful way to grow your money over time and increase your wealth.

Analyst and traders look at all kinds of information before they speculate (educated guess) on the direction of individual stocks, sectors, or markets. That speculation plays out every day causing the ups and downs of stock markets all over the world. Sometimes those "psychics" are right and sometimes they are wrong. It doesn't really matter to the informed investor because we know that we are investing for the long-term. The short-term is irrelevant and we know it.

Over time, markets adjust toward their proper valuations within each market; we just don't know when. That's why we ignore the daily ups and downs. Informed investors focus on earnings and dividends, not what people think will happen.

(3) Investing in stocks is a rigged game that the average investor cannot win. There is some truth to that final point. Like many things in American society, systems gradually move in a direction to help the wealthy, the powerful, and the well-connected, but thanks to John Bogle, **you and I can benefit from that rigged game by owning entire markets at a very low cost** (no-load index mutual funds).

Investing in the stock market is a very wise move based on the historical returns (slightly more than 10% per year before costs over the last 90 years). This provides you a positive real return that few other investments can provide.

The key to investing in stocks is to do it at a small cost as you diversify your stock investments all over the world, which will in turn reduce your risk of temporary and permanent loss. This is how you become the wise and successful investor.

"We can use historical data to answer a simple question: Why have stocks provided long-term real returns of 7 percent? Answer: Almost entirely because of the rising earnings and dividends of U.S. corporations."

- **John Bogle**, *Common Sense on Mutual Funds*

48

BONDS

When you buy bonds (also called *fixed income*), you are buying debt. The wise and successful investor owns debt, rather than accumulating it as they focus on diversification, income, and liquidity.

A bond is issued for many reasons, but primarily, to raise money. The organization who issues the bond promises to pay a certain interest rate if you hold that bond to maturity, which could be 2 years, 5 years, 10 years, or maybe 30 years. Why should you invest in bonds?

Diversification, income and liquidity are very good reasons. Bonds provide a cushion in your portfolio when stocks go down and that will happen at different periods of time. In many cases, bonds go up when stocks go down (high quality bonds performed quite well in 2008 when stocks collapsed). This makes them negatively correlated to stocks (more on that later in the book as we delve into asset allocation).

Income is another really good reason. Bonds with different maturities and quality pay out different rates of interest (*yield*). That interest provides income during good times and most importantly, the bad.

Liquidity provides you easy access to your bonds as they are traded on the open market. In a nutshell, holding a large amount of bonds in a mutual fund will provide you all the liquidity you will need.

What types of bonds should you own? The advice doesn't change much from stocks. Own a lot of quality bonds in no-load index mutual funds. This will diversify you in government and corporate bonds all over the United States and the world (not required) at rock-bottom costs.

Own thousands of bonds in a bond mutual fund rather than two or three. The Total Bond Market Index Fund at Vanguard owns over 7000 individual bonds. That is diversification! You can do your own research on which bond fund is right for you. Own one or more short- to intermediate-bond funds and do it at the lowest possible cost, then move on.

Quality bonds? No junk! Junk bonds (also called high-yield bonds) pay higher interest on their debt because they are more likely to not pay out based on their past performance and future possibilities (they could stiff you). Here is my simple advice when it comes to junk. DO NOT own high-yield bonds. You don't need them.

Focus on owning bonds with maturities below 10 years and strive to get those maturities down to 5 years as best you can. Why? The lower the maturity, the less the bond is affected by rising interest rates. The goal is not to take a great deal of risk with bonds. Take your risks with stocks.

What is the historical return on bonds? It is about 5% for intermediate bonds. That is before costs. A good bond index fund should cost you .3% or less. That Total Bond Market Index Fund at Vanguard will cost you .07% for Admiral Shares. Try to find similar bond index funds in your retirement accounts at work.

Here is the bottom line on bonds. Bonds are less risky than stocks; therefore, they end up paying a lower return (10% vs. 5% roughly). Buy them to reduce the risk in your portfolio while adding income.

"… you get the most "bang for the buck" by about a five-year maturity. This is the steepest part of the yield curve—the part that rewards you the most. Beyond that, the extra return diminishes, with continually increasing risk. The stock portion of your portfolio is the place to take risk, not the bond portion, where the purpose is to shelter you from market downturns and provide ready liquidity."

- **William Bernstein,** *The Four Pillars of Investing*

49

THE RULE OF 72

The Rule of 72 is a very important concept to understand. It will provide you a platform as you build upon your knowledge about the world of investing. By understanding this rule, you will better appreciate why you must take risk with your investment dollars. Risk and return are connected just like your hand is connected to your arm. The sooner you learn that very important idea, the quicker you will start to see your portfolio grow.

The Rule of 72 tells us how long it will take to double your money based on the rate of return of your investments. You take 72 and divide it by the amount of interest you are earning (let's say 8%) and that will tell you how many years before your money will double. In this case, it would take 9 years (72 divided by 8 = 9 years).

Here is an example: You have $10,000. At 8%, that money will double to $20,000 in 9 years. Then, that $20,000 will double to $40,000 in another 9 years (18 years in total). **You would have $160,000 in 36 years at that pace!** I think you can see how this compounding effect can grow a portfolio pretty darn fast, but here is the caveat. You have to take risk to earn 8%. You have to be willing to see your portfolio go down in value in the short-term so it will grow over the long-term. Risk = return.

Does risk scare you? It scares me, but keeping the money in the "safe" bank and earning 1% is not the solution (that interest rate is a bit high with the current low interest rate environment in 2015 where many people are not even earning .2%). Using the rule of 72, it will take you 72 years to reach $20,000 with your $10,000 at 1%. When considering the return you want on your money, you must decide how much risk you are willing to take. Little to no risk gets you little to no return.

At 1%, you would have $20,000 in 72 years.

At 8%, you would have $2,560,000 in 72 years.

Which would you prefer?

That's a silly question, isn't it? We all would like the 8% return, but the short-term risk is tough to swallow for many of us. I get that, and I don't like to see my portfolio go down in value either, but if you and I want that 8% return, we must be willing to see drops in our investment portfolio during any given time period.

Now let's look at a couple nuances that we should consider when using this rule. When factoring in your average return, make sure you account for costs (commissions, loads, fees, etc.) and taxes. You want to achieve an 8% return after costs (no-load index mutual funds for the informed investor) and after taxes (keep the money in retirement accounts at work and outside of work in Roth IRAs as best you can).

That average return is going to fluctuate in some pretty big ways over the years. You might see yearly returns that look like these: 8%, 27%, 2%, -13%, 10%, -5%, 16%, and 19%. Every year your portfolio will produce a different return. The informed investor accepts volatility.

Markets don't go up forever and they don't go down forever. It's the average return *after costs* we are focused on and the one we can use when applying the Rule of 72 to better understand the value of taking risk as we seek higher returns on our money. Know your math!

"You do not get something for nothing. Investors who take no investment risk should expect no return after adjusting for inflation and taxes. …taking investment risk also means that you can and will lose money at times. There is simply no way around this. There is no free lunch."

- **Rick Ferri**, *All About Asset Allocation*

50

OPPORTUNITY COST

There is thing called *opportunity cost* and it is vital that you understand this concept and how to apply it to your life. When you allocate money in one place, it's not going somewhere else. That is the simple version of opportunity cost. Now let's see how it can be applied to real life in some very tangible ways.

Let's say you have a mortgage with an interest rate of 4%. If you have extra money that you can allocate elsewhere, do you put it toward the mortgage at 4% or your investments in retirement accounts like a 401(k) or a Roth IRA? Basically, what is the opportunity cost that you will incur by making one move instead of another?

First, do you know how to earn more than 4% on your investments after costs? Sadly, I think most people do not. If that were the case, I would put the extra money toward the mortgage. If you know how to create a portfolio of no-load index mutual funds (explained later in the book), then investing the money would be the wiser move. Let's take a look.

Earning an estimated 8% after costs on your investments trumps the 4% you would earn by paying the mortgage debt off early, and it's not really that close. The mortgage may even give you a slight tax deduction, as well, making the decision even easier.

Tax sheltering the investments in retirement accounts is also a very wise move. So, if you paid down the mortgage early at 4%, you have lost the opportunity to make 8% on your investments. That is opportunity cost. You should consider opportunity cost with every financial decision you make while educating yourself all along the way.

As with all cases, there are nuances to the issue. Let's say you have a 10% interest rate on a loan, and based on your asset allocation of stock and bond index mutual funds, you don't see the likelihood of a return beyond 8%. You would pay the loan before investing, right? Not necessarily.

If you are looking at your retirement plan at work and there is matching money involved, I would not bypass that very good deal. Not investing there would miss out on a 100% return on that FREE matching money. That is an opportunity you cannot pass up! Capture the free money and then go back and pay extra on that 10% loan.

Here is another distinction. You have identified the investment option to be the better one over the mortgage option, but instead of investing the money, you spend it. Now you are out the 8% AND the 4%, and you have little to nothing to show for it. In that case, you would have been better off putting the money toward the 4% mortgage.

There are other considerations. Sometimes we make decisions that may not be best financially, but they are right on a psychological level. You may incur less stress (debt weighs heavily on some people) by paying down the 4% mortgage even though it would be wiser financially to put the money toward your 8% expected return on your investments.

Sometimes, that may be the best option in some circumstances for some people. Just make sure you understand what you are giving up in opportunity cost when making a decision like that. Know your opportunities and act accordingly.

"Lost in a sea of misinformation, investors float and drift hither and yon, reaping poor results. Using either no strategy or a fatally flawed approach, the overwhelming majority of investors place their meager and hard-earned savings in the wrong markets and then fail to even come close to a market return."

- **Frank Armstrong III**, *The Informed Investor*

51

THE MARKET

You are going to hear a lot about "the market" as you continue your reading. It's probably wise to clearly define this "thing" before moving forward. When someone references the market, they could be referring to the Dow Jones Industrials, the S&P 500, the Wilshire 5000, the Russell 3000, the NASDAQ 100, the MSCI EAFE, or possibly the Barclay's U.S. Aggregate (bonds), to name just a few.

That's quite a list, right? At any given time, someone might be referring to one or more of those markets when they say "the market." So how do you know which one they are talking about? It's not always easy. Let's take a step back and consider a few things.

Under many circumstances, the market is used to describe the U.S. stock market. This would include small, medium, and large companies. The best benchmarks that track the entire market would be the Wilshire 5000 and the Russell 3000. And yet, the S&P 500 (the Standard and Poor's representation of 500 of the largest publicly traded companies in the U.S.) tends to be the most widely referenced benchmark. Why?

Some benchmarks are much better known than others (the S&P 500 for example) and they do a pretty good job of capturing much of the total market return (about 80%). The S&P 500 also provides results that go back many decades so it's easy to research it over long periods of time.

There is a problem though. The S&P 500 benchmark does not account for medium and small companies (about 20% of the U.S. market). The Wilshire 5000 and the Russell 3000 does account for those. This is why they are better benchmarks when looking at the entire U.S. economy.

What about the Dow Jones Industrial Average (the Dow)? This index is a poor representation of the market. It tracks only 30 of the largest companies in America. So why do you hear about it so much? It's old and it's something that has been reported on for what appears to be forever. Tradition dies very slowly, even on Wall Street. I would recommend you ignore the Dow. It means nothing to the long-term investor.

This discussion has yet to talk about the world stock market indices. If we wanted a benchmark for that, we would probably reference the MSCI World benchmark index that captures developed and developing countries all over the world.

What about a benchmark for the world stock and bond markets? Is there one of them? Yep. The MSCI Global Capital Markets Index provides a global index for the investor who wants to track asset classes all over the world. As you can see, this subject gets more complicated as we dig deeper into "the market."

So what is the point of all of this? It is important to know what someone means when they are talking about the market. You should inquire which market they are referencing and why they chose that particular one. Many times they aren't sure or they are simply repeating something someone else said.

The informed investor will also see through the marketing used by many advisors when they brag about beating the market. Which market did they beat? Here is another one of those dirty little secrets. Many managed funds compare themselves to the S&P 500 even though they own many small companies. This is false advertising. Know your markets!

"More often than not, an advisor who is showing high returns relative to a benchmark is using an inappropriate benchmark that they know is easy to beat. If this benchmark begins to perform better than the advisor, the advisor changes benchmarks."

- **Rick Ferri**, *The Power of Passive Investing*

52

THE INDEX FUND

The publicly-traded index fund was the creation of John Bogle. Back in 1975, Mr. Bogle changed the landscape of investing forever and thanks to him, you and I have been provided a wonderful way to invest our money all over the world at a very low cost.

What is an index fund? It is a mutual fund that owns stocks and/or bonds that mimic a particular index. The Vanguard 500 Index Fund is a good example. This index mimics the S&P 500, which represents 500 of the largest companies in the United States.

There are many types of index funds. Some index funds track a developed international market, a developing international market, or maybe a small-cap U.S. market like the Russell 2000. There are also many index funds that track bond markets in the United States and abroad. The list is almost endless.

So which ones should you own and why? It depends of course, based on your particular situation. A good rule to follow would start you off with a total U.S. stock market index fund that owns all or almost all of the publicly traded companies in America. This is a wonderful way to diversify you over a big swath of the world economy.

You would then consider adding a total international stock index fund and then you might start breaking it down even further from there as you own an emerging markets index fund, a REIT index fund, a small-cap value index fund, a large-cap value index fund, and it is always wise to own one or more bond index funds in the U.S. and/or overseas. Does that sound a bit intimidating?

You could disregard owning individual index mutual funds and instead, own Target Date Retirement Funds that invest in multiple index funds. **This will diversify you all over the world with one fund!**

Many people like the idea of owning one fund, and there is absolutely no reason why you shouldn't consider that. There is a list of recommended index funds that follow this chapter. Take your time, research them, and select the fund(s) that are right for you. Now let's look at some problems with index investing.

Many index funds charge you a load to own them. You should NEVER pay a load to invest with an index fund. If you avoid those "helpers" and stick with index funds at your workplace and Vanguard, you should accomplish that.

Many index funds have been created so an individual can use them in a tactical way. Tactical way? They buy an index fund that specializes in a specific industry, country, or asset class as they attempt to predict the future. That is a terrible idea. When buying index funds, focus on broadly diversified funds that you buy and hold for long periods of time.

Not all index funds are cheap. If you are paying more than .5% (yearly expense ratio) for an index fund, you are paying too much. Those yearly fees should fall under .3% (also called 30 basis points) and you should strive to get them down to .1% per year. The lower those fees go, the higher the returns will be for you in your future.

"Beware: Some index funds charge unconscionably high management fees. We believe you should buy only those domestic common-stock funds that charge one-fifth of 1 percent or less annually as management expenses. And while the fees for investing in international funds tend to be higher than for U.S. funds, we believe you should limit yourself to the lowest-cost international index funds as well."

- **Burton Malkiel and Charles Ellis**, *The Elements of Investing*

Recommended Index Mutual Funds

Go to vanguard.com to learn more. Admiral Shares require a minimum investment of $10,000.

Stock Index Funds (Admiral Shares)	Expense Ratio
Total Stock Market Index Fund	.05%
500 Index Fund	.05%
Total International Stock Index Fund	.14%
Emerging Markets Stock Index Fund	.15%
REIT Index Fund	.10%
Small-Cap Value Index Fund	.09%
Value Index Fund	.09%

Bond Index Funds (Admiral Shares)	Expense Ratio
Total Bond Market Index Fund	.07%
Short-Term Bond Index Fund	.10%
Total International Bond Index Fund	.19%

Target Date Retirement Funds	Expense Ratio
Target Date Retirement Funds 2010-2060	.16% − .18%

53

VANGUARD

You have heard me go on and on about Vanguard. I would like to take a moment and again remind you that Vanguard *does not* pay me. I seriously doubt they know who I am, and that's okay. I just hope they keep doing business the way they have done it in the past.

I recommend Vanguard for some very good reasons. One, I have been investing with them for over 20 years, and they have exceeded my expectations time and again. This not-for-profit company started by John Bogle provides a long list of no-load index mutual funds at very low yearly fees. Unlike most investment companies, the fees drop as more money comes in. That is not the norm in this industry.

Vanguard has been around for quite some time. They currently have over $3 trillion dollars under management. Those are big numbers! When you start to ask how they make money when their index funds are so cheap, consider that $3 trillion number. If they end up making .5% per year on that number, they are doing mighty well. The volume has helped them keep the prices low, and thanks to John Bogle, the business model has been set up to benefit the client, rather than exploit him/her.

Vanguard also offers no-load annuities that are quite cheap by annuity standards (about .5% per year). If you have an annuity now, I would recommend moving it to Vanguard via a 1035 exchange to reduce your yearly fees (if the plan is qualified you might be able to turn it into a Traditional IRA and totally discharge the annuity part). Most annuities have yearly costs that run around 2% or more. Just be careful to avoid any surrender penalties. Take your time to understand what you are doing and why you are doing it when making this move.

As I stated in a previous chapter, I only recommend a small number of funds at Vanguard. Most of Vanguard's funds should be avoided. Why? They will cost you more money than the index funds and give you a lower probability of higher returns over time.

This issue is not that complicated. Actively managed mutual funds (even the cheap ones at Vanguard) cost more, and those costs reduce your final return little by little with each passing year. Fees matter. They always have and they always will.

Are there other families that do a good job? Sure, but I don't entirely trust them. Many investment companies have turned into very large marketing companies. They create funds and then promote the dickens out of them. Just say no to the pretty commercials and slick marketing techniques. Those boring index funds at Vanguard will serve you just fine.

If you use a fee-only advisor (discussed later in the book), Vanguard funds may or may not be an option. DFA (Dimensional Fund Advisors) could be a smart option for many. Why? They are slightly more expensive than the Vanguard funds, but they are very focused on using the peer-reviewed research as they invest your money passively with a tilt in your portfolio toward small and value companies.

Now what? As always, fall back on education. Do your own research before making changes to your portfolio. Identify the truth (identify the true color of the sky) as you shuffle through the minutia of advertising spewed out to cloud the truth. Higher returns will follow.

"More often the conclusions (supporting active management) can only be justified by assuming that the laws of arithmetic have been suspended for the convenience of those who choose to pursue careers as active managers."

- **William F. Sharpe**, Nobel Laureate in Economics

54

THE OTHERS

So I just got done telling you how great Vanguard is when it comes to investing your money. What about other investment companies? Don't other companies offer really cheap index mutual funds? Yes they do, but there are a few issues to discuss before considering those other companies.

Let's take Fidelity. Fidelity is a big boy in the business of investing, and they offer just as many good no-load index mutual funds as Vanguard with some very comparable expense ratios. If you focused solely on those index funds at Fidelity, you would be just fine, but there is a problem that you must be aware of when investing at a place like Fidelity.

Fidelity offers many *load* mutual funds. They also offer many *managed* mutual funds. Both of those types of funds will cost you a great deal more in yearly costs. I am wary of companies like Fidelity because they might pull the industries version of a bait and switch on you.

Here is how it works. They offer the cheap index funds that are basically identical to the index funds at Vanguard. That is the bait. They pull you in like a grocery store pulls you in with a cheap gallon of milk or loaf of bread. Once you are in, they start selling you other items that are much more profitable for the business. That is the switch.

It can be very effective. You move your money to Fidelity and into index funds. Soon after, you start getting messages from the company telling you how this mutual fund and that mutual fund has beaten its index over different time periods. At this point you're thinking, "What the hell." I thought index funds were the best. So you switch to the "better" mutual funds. When you do that, you are chasing performance. That's not good.

The investment company is calling the Super Bowl after the game has been played. Anyone can tell you who won *last year's* Super Bowl. That takes a simple Google search to find out. The difficult part is predicting who will win *next* year's Super Bowl. Most people will get that wrong.

Many investment companies trot out the winning mutual funds from the previous year(s) knowing that will impress some people. "Look Mom, a five-star rating!" That reflects the past, not the future. When you fall for that pitch, you are being overly influenced by the small amount of winners while you are not informed on the large amount of losers.

In any given time period anyone can identify actively-managed mutual funds that beat their benchmark indexes. It's not that hard. I can do that. That doesn't mean anything. Identifying who won the Super Bowl after the game has been played is easy. Predicting who will win the game next year is very hard. That's why we invest in no-load index mutual funds.

The probabilities are on our side when we select index funds. It is probable that your index funds will beat most active managed mutual funds. It is possible for some of those managed funds to beat their benchmark indexes. The informed investor focuses on the probabilities over the possibilities.

I stick with Vanguard because they have no track record of marketing their five-star funds to their unsuspecting index investors. That's good enough for me, and I think it's good enough for you. Scrutinize very carefully before selecting an investment management company. They may or may not be on your side.

"Getting an unsophisticated client was the golden prize. The quickest way to make money on Wall Street is to take the most sophisticated product and try to sell it to the least sophisticated client."

- **Goldman Sachs VP** explains why he quit

55

TAXES

You should always consider taxes when investing your money. Many people don't, and they end up paying more tax than they should. For example, if you own managed mutual funds outside of retirement, you are paying more taxes because of the high turnover (a lot of buying and selling).

That doesn't mean that taxes should be the driving force with each investment decision you make, but it does mean you should consider the tax consequences with each decision along the way. Why? **It can save you a great deal of money!** Follow the advice below and you will pay less tax on your dividends as well (they become qualified dividends if held for a period extending beyond 60 days).

Here are some basics. Short-term capital gains (securities held for one year or less) should be avoided as best you can as you reach for long-term capital gains (securities held for more than one year). Why? Short-term capital gains are taxed like ordinary income. Long-term capital gains are taxed at much lower rates, and it's possible you could pay 0%!

How does a person accrue capital gains? When securities are sold for a profit, you will have a capital gain. The length you owned that security determines whether it a short-term or long-term capital gain. Buying and holding your investments with index funds for long periods of time will load you up with long-term capital gains. Next up are tax-efficient funds.

What makes an investment tax-efficient? An investment that has low turnover (minimal buying and selling) will reduce the costs to manage the fund and that should reduce your annual expense ratio. Index funds not only reduce your yearly expenses, but they also reduce your tax bill.

This discussion is solely focused on funds outside your retirement accounts. You can eliminate or defer tax when investing in retirement accounts [a 401(k) or a Roth IRA, for example], which you should strive to do until you hit the yearly contribution limits on each type of account. Here are the rules for long-term capital gains for the 2015 tax year.

- If you are in the 39.6% tax bracket, you will pay 20% on your long-term capital gains.
- If you are in the 35%, 33%, 28%, or 25% tax brackets, you will pay 15% on your long-term capital gains.
- If you are in the **15% or 10% tax brackets,** you will pay **0%** on your **long-term capital gains!**

When investing outside of retirement accounts, select broadly diversified no-load index mutual funds like these two Vanguard funds: Total Stock Market Index Fund and the Total International Stock Index Fund. Adjust your portfolio appropriately (speak to your accountant as needed before making any buying or selling decisions).

What are the less tax-efficient funds? Bond funds and large dividend paying stock funds like a REIT Index Fund would fall into this category. Basically, anything that produces a high amount of yearly income should be held inside retirement accounts when possible. You have more control over how your investments are taxed than you might realize. Take control!

"Passive investing may have the "disadvantage" of being boring. However, it guarantees that you receive market returns in a low-cost and tax-efficient manner if you have the discipline to adhere to your investment policy statement. It also frees you from spending any time at all watching CNBC, studying charts, following Internet discussion sites, and reading financial publications that are basically not much more than the equivalent of astrology."

- **Larry Swedroe**, *The Quest for Alpha*

56

THE ROTH IRA

The Roth IRA is a wonderful vehicle to use when investing in those very efficient no-load index mutual funds. Sometimes it is hard for people to totally understand what a Roth IRA is and so here is a simple illustration that I hope will help.

Think of a Roth IRA as a car. Now think of the people who ride in that car. The people go by the name of no-load index mutual funds. When you put the people in the car, they are protected from injury.

That protection provides safety (from taxes with a Roth IRA). Everyone who has earned income should consider having a Roth IRA. Now let's take a look at some of the rules that pertain to a Roth IRA.

(1) You have to have earned income to contribute to a Roth IRA (can be circumvented for some non-working spouses).

(2) You can only contribute a certain amount (that is $5,500 for people under age 50 and $6,500 for people 50 years and older in 2015).

(3) There are income limits. (they start at $114,000 for single people and $181,000 for married people who file jointly in 2015).

You must wait five years from your first contribution before taking out earnings tax-free. You must wait until age 59.5 to avoid taxes and penalties on those earnings (there are exceptions). Now let's take a look at some benefits.

The contributions you place in the account can be taken out anytime in the future without penalty or taxes. Yes, you read that right. Any money you contribute, you can take out any time in the future without penalties or taxes no matter what your age. The first money you take out of Roth IRAs will always be your contributions. Earnings come out when the contributions have dried up.

As stated earlier, the earnings will grow tax-free. After age 59.5, you can access that money and NEVER pay federal or state income tax! There is no RMD (required minimum distribution) on Roth IRAs. This means when you hit age 70.5, you will not have to take money out of the account as you do with pre-tax retirement accounts. You also have up to April 15th of the following year to contribute to your previous year's Roth IRA.

Where should you open a Roth IRA? This is pretty easy. Go to vanguard.com and select no-load index mutual funds (minimum investment is $3,000) or target date retirement funds that own index mutual funds (minimum investment is $1,000). You can own one fund or a few. Make sure the funds you select make sense for your situation. Consider all other investments (in your retirement plan at work, for example) before selecting investments for your Roth IRA (proper asset allocation is the reason).

Your options are almost endless. Educate yourself. Identify your particular situation, consider your options, and act, by making the move toward opening a Roth IRA. Finally, keep feeding it month after month and year after year. Financial freedom is sure to follow!

"Deep down, I remain absolutely confident that the vast majority of American families will be well served by owning their equity holdings in an all –U.S. stock-market index portfolio and holding their bonds in an all-U.S. bond-market index portfolio. …The rationale for a 100-percent-index-fund portfolio remains as solid as a rock. It's all about common sense."

- **John Bogle**, *The Little Book of Common Sense Investing*

57

TRADITIONAL OR ROTH?

When investing your money at the workplace, many of you will have the option of selecting a traditional defined contribution plan [401(k), 403(b), TSP, and 457(b), for example] or the Roth version. I call these "freedom" plans. By saving and investing wisely in these type of plans, you will provide yourself the opportunity to retire one day with the freedom to do whatever it is you want to do with the rest of your life.

Which one should you select if both options are offered at your current company? "It depends" is the right answer, and that means you need to answer a couple of questions. The issue primarily hinges on taxes and how much you're currently making in gross earnings. Let's explore the issue before making a decision just yet.

First, the traditional plan. Money goes in *before* it is taxed. This can reduce your federal and state income taxes in the year in which you contribute. For example, you make $50,000 in gross income. If you invest $10,000 in a traditional plan, you will be taxed on $40,000 ($50,000 - $10,000). If your combined marginal federal and state income tax bracket is 25%, you will have deferred (delayed paying the tax) $2,500 ($10,000 minus 25%) in tax. That is nice, but is it smart?

Now let's look at the Roth version. You make the same $50,000, but you select the Roth, which moves the money in *after* tax. There is no immediate tax benefit. You will be taxed on that $50,000 in the year that you earn it, but when you pull that money out many years later, and you follow the rules, ALL of it (including the earnings) will be tax-free. That is quite a benefit, and you should consider it. Those earnings will be taxed later down the road as earned income if you select the traditional version.

So what should you consider when deciding between a Traditional or a Roth? First, let's start with your tax situation. You want to consider federal, state, and city income tax when making this very important decision. Do you live in a state that has a high state and/or city income tax? If so, the traditional version gets a bump up in consideration. If not, it gets a bump down. Once you have identified your marginal tax rate (how your last dollar is taxed), take a look at your gross income.

How much is your yearly gross income? You will want to consider your family's gross income when making this decision. Here is a basic rule of thumb that I use (consider everything, not just this recommendation). If you are single and pay federal and state income tax, consider the traditional version if you make over $60,000. If you don't pay state income tax, I would bump that number up to $80,000. If you earn under those amounts as a single person, I would consider the Roth version.

If your family's gross income were equal to those amounts, I would definitely consider the Roth version. You will not be getting much of a tax break by selecting the traditional plan. Here is a rule of thumb for married people. If your family's gross income is under $100,000, the Roth version is probably the wise choice even if you pay federal and state income tax. If you only pay federal, you might consider raising that amount to $120,000 when making this decision.

Ultimately, you will need to make these decisions yourself. Just be careful not to make them in a vacuum (consider the whole family situation when deciding on the right option). Also keep in mind you can always do one or the other as time goes on and your situation changes. You can also do both at the same time if you want to hedge your bets against an uncertain future. As always, educate and act on what you learn.

"Inaction breeds doubt and fear. Action breeds confidence and courage. If you want to conquer fear, do not sit home and think about it. Go out and get busy."

- **Dale Carnegie**, Writer and Lecturer

58

INVESTING FOR COLLEGE

I know many parents went straight to this chapter, and I understand why. This is a big deal! College can be very, very expensive and if you wait until your child starts going to school, you will have missed the opportunities that come with compound interest.

If you have kids, start saving NOW. Use information contained in this book and on my website, thecrazymaninthepinkwig.com, to start investing for your child's education. You have many options, but I feel three options should be considered above all others.

The **529 College Plan** can be a great choice for many. There will be a state tax deduction for most and tax-free withdrawals for those that follow the rules carefully. Let's get right to the chase on the investment part of it. NEVER use a financial advisor when investing in a 529 Plan. Go straight to the state when opening this type of account.

Always consider costs as you select the plan that is right for you. The goal should be to find a plan that has the lowest costs with multiple investing options (preferably index funds). I would not pay more than .3% per year. If your state plan has higher costs than that, I would consider another state plan (of course, you should consider the tax deduction prior to making this decision to switch plans).

I would look at the age-based tracks first. Most plans have one or more of these options. Age-based plans invest for your child based on their current age. When they are under two years old for example, they will be invested heavily in stocks. As your child gets older, the fund moves to more bonds and cash. This rebalancing happens without any effort on your part.

Another option could be a **Roth IRA**. If you feel like your company retirement plan will suffice in retirement (it will take quite a commitment from you to make that happen), you could allocate your Roth IRA and your spouse's Roth IRA to your child's education. Think this through carefully before choosing this option.

Where do you go for your Roth IRA? This is easy. Go to vanguard.com and open up a target date retirement fund that equals your child's first year in college. For example, if your child would enter college in the year 2030, select the Target Retirement 2025 or 2030 Fund. It will gradually rebalance over time, making it more conservative (more bonds and less stocks). This will diversify you over stock and bond markets all over the world at a very low cost (.18% or less).

The third option is that same **Target Date Retirement Fund** outside of your Roth IRA. Why? This gives you more options. The 529 Plan and the Roth IRA come with a great deal of restrictions and rules. A taxable Target Date Retirement Fund gives you more freedom when you end up taking the money out at a later date. You can use it for college or for other purposes that have nothing to do with education. I would definitely make sure the money was in the adults name. I would not trust an 18 year old with large chunks of money. That brain is not fully developed.

Here is the final takeaway on investing for college. Get started immediately once you have educated yourself on your options and selected the one that fits your situation best. Your child will be college age before you know it. Keep feeding the account AND remind other family members they are welcome to do the same by placing money in the fund directly or handing over a gift to you to contribute into the account.

"The stock market is a highly efficient mechanism for the transfer of wealth from the impatient to the patient."

- **Warren Buffett**

59

INVESTING FOR RETIREMENT

This chapter primarily deals with your company retirement plan at work for employees [small business owners can open up individual 401(k) accounts or a SEP-IRA]. This should not be the only place you invest. Consider a Roth IRA and taxable accounts outside of work as well.

Your company retirement plan is designed to help you save for your future retirement needs. They go by different numbers and initials based on what kind of employer you work for. This discussion deals with the defined contribution plans (you are the primary contributor). If you have a defined benefit plan (pension), count your lucky stars. Most people don't.

The 401(k) is for individuals who work for private and public corporations. The 403(b) is for non-profits, which would include many teachers and private charities throughout the country. State workers will have a 457(b). Finally, the TSP (Thrift Savings Plan) is for federal workers. These plans are primarily the same, but the options can vary dramatically.

Identify index funds or Target Date Retirement Funds when possible. This requires you to review the investments offered with great care. It is critical that you take control of the situation and that means understanding what options are available to you AND at what cost (know the fees per each investment).

Take as much time as you need as you identify the expense ratio (the fees) that goes with each fund. Focus on investments that cost you .3% or less. This would take you to index funds. If your company does not offer any options that are inexpensive, you need to start complaining until they do. Get some co-workers to join you!

Once you identify the inexpensive funds, then you want to identify what the default fund is with your plan. The default fund is where your initial investments go. That's not where you want to keep your money in many cases.

The default fund is usually a low-risk money market fund or short-maturity bond fund. Your money will not grow beyond inflation with these types of funds. Consider moving your money and future contributions to one or more stock index funds instead.

Some companies have started changing the default fund to a Target Date Retirement Fund that matches your estimated retirement date. This could be a good option for many, BUT make sure those types of funds are inexpensive (below .3%). Many are not. Most of the hard stuff has been done when you have completed these steps. Now it's time to feed them!

You want to **capture all matching money** from your employer. It's free and that is a 100% return. Go get it! You also want to consider increasing your contribution amounts over time as you save more and more into your selected funds. Here is a simple rule of thumb. Start with saving 10% and increase it every year by 2%. The money will come out automatically, which will make it painless. Now let's cover what not to do.

- DO NOT invest in individual stock (see Enron for an example).
- DO NOT trade in and out of your retirement plan.
- DO NOT borrow against your plan (you are stealing from YOU).
- DO NOT cash it out when you leave (transfer it to an IRA).
- DO NOT make this decision without considering other investments you have outside of work.

"First, get diversified. Come up with a portfolio that covers a lot of asset classes. Second, you want to keep your fees low. That means avoiding the most hyped but expensive funds, in favor of low-cost index funds."

- **Jack Meyer,** Former Manager of the Harvard Investment Company

60

INVESTING IN RETIREMENT

Notice the small difference that defines this chapter from the last. Investing *in* retirement is a subject that is rarely discussed and often misunderstood. I am going to state something obvious (at least I hope so). It is very important to not only save and invest for your retirement needs, but it is just as important to invest wisely while you in retirement.

Far too many people want to move all of their investments to bonds, cash, and annuities when they retire. That is a mistake. You need growth in retirement and that means stocks. Now I am not saying you need to have as much in stocks as when you were a young person, but a healthy amount is warranted to keep your portfolio growing. How much?

(1) Are your investments solely for you or is some of your portfolio earmarked for your heirs?

(2) How much of your investment money do you need per year to supplement your other money like pensions, Social Security, and annuities?

(3) How much risk can you tolerate without it making your heart race and forcing a trip to the hospital?

Here is a rule of thumb. Keep at least 30% of your portfolio in stocks. Go up to 50% or more if you are expecting to be in retirement for a long time and/or you intend to leave money to others. Are those numbers exact? No. Each situation is different, but it helps to have a reference point.

You would be wise to select individual index funds to accomplish these allocations or you could select one or more Target Date Retirement Funds at Vanguard to simplify the matter. Keeping your costs down will keep your investments growing at a greater rate long into retirement. I hope that is becoming quite obvious at this point.

This issue becomes much more complicated as you start to consider all other matters outside of your investments. A good fee-only financial planner (discussed in a later chapter) could help you in many ways beyond what I am trying to do with this chapter. They can assist you with Social Security issues, insurance needs, estate planning, and much, much more.

The primary point of this chapter is to make you aware that you should still take risk with stocks long into retirement if you want that money to last. The efficient frontier (trying to capture an expected return with a certain level of risk) can help you better understand the importance of keeping stocks in your portfolio for a very long time. Google "efficient frontier" if you would like to understand this concept better.

Diversification is a critical component of any portfolio. The simplest and most effective method for most would be an all index portfolio that owns markets all over the world at a very low cost. I would encourage you to read Daniel Solin's book, *The Smartest Retirement Book You'll Ever Read*, to further your education on this matter.

"The transition from working to retirement is an uncertain time. Accordingly, a retiree's portfolio should be managed with stability and safety of principal as its primary objectives. However, a retirement portfolio still needs growth. A person at age 65 is likely to live for 20 more years, according to IRS Publication 590. As such, the median asset allocation for people in early retirement is 50 percent in stocks and 50 percent in fixed income."

- Rick Ferri, *All About Asset Allocation*

61

TRANSFERRING MONEY

The day will come when you will need to transfer your money from one institution to another. Maybe you will transfer money out of your 401(k) from your old job. Maybe you have "seen the light" and decided to move your investments away from your local broker or fee-based financial advisor and into those very efficient no-load index mutual funds at Vanguard. It's time for action!

This will require a bit of paperwork on your part. You must be willing, able, and knowledgeable about what you are doing when you start moving money around. You also want to avoid penalties and taxes as you move retirement accounts from one place to another.

There is a great deal of money at stake, and I can promise you the financial industry and its "helpers" know this all too well. I recommend you move your money to Vanguard when that time comes.

The people at Vanguard will spend the needed time with you as you follow through on the process. They will make sure the paperwork is filled out correctly. They will answer your questions, and they do this at no cost. How do I know? I have done it, and I have helped hundreds of other people do it. You can do it.

It is important that you put together a plan that reduces investment costs and taxes when you transfer your money. Many people have multiple retirement accounts doing little or nothing because they have been neglected over time. Find out exactly where those funds are, how you can access them, and when you can start taking action to get YOUR money under YOUR control. It's YOUR money. Don't ever forget that.

Why should you do a transfer? It is in your best interest, that's why. Whether you are forced to take action (you quit, were fired, retire, etc.) or you have simply identified a better option (no-load index mutual funds), it benefits you to move your money to a place where you are in control of it. This is why you should transfer money to a place like Vanguard. Paying no commission or load is another pretty big deal. Let's take a look.

Let's say a financial advisor is going to "help" you transfer $100,000 from your current retirement account to a managed load mutual fund. With a 5.75% class A load, you would pay $5,750. That money goes to the salesperson, not the mutual fund. By avoiding the middleman, you can put the entire $100,000 into the no-load index mutual funds that fit your needs. You benefit by taking control of the situation. You end up keeping:

$5,750!

You also reduce your yearly fees with those very efficient and inexpensive index mutual funds. You could save 2% or more in fees and loads per year by focusing on an all index no-load portfolio. With education, this becomes a very logical move.

Take the time to understand what you are doing, and only transfer money when you know why you are doing it, where it is going, and how much it will cost you. It's time to take control of YOUR money!

"It's fun to play around...it's human nature to try to select the right horse...(But) for the average person, I'm more of an indexer...The predictability is so high...For 10, 15, 20 years you'll be in the 85th percentile of performance. Why would you screw it up?"

- Charles Schwab

62

INVESTING IN REAL ESTATE

You might recognize that I have a strong bias toward investing in stock and bond markets. You would be right about that. Thanks to index funds, you and I can do it at a very low cost (under .3% per year). I choose not to invest with rental real estate like many do.

I choose to invest in publicly-traded REITs (stock in commercial real estate like malls and commercial buildings) rather than rental real estate. The yearly returns are similar but the costs will favor a diversified publicly traded REIT index fund like the one at Vanguard. Let's take a look.

You can make a case that a person who knows what they are doing could earn a 9% yearly return on real estate that produces income. This applies to REITs (that produce yearly earnings and dividends) and rental properties (that produce yearly appreciation and rent). If the REITs cost you .1%, your after cost return is 8.9%. That's not bad.

What will your yearly costs equal with rental real estate? Many people do a poor job of tracking that number. They tend to track the monthly cash flow, yearly rent, and maybe the appreciation of the property, but the total costs tend to get lost in the shuffle. It is important to consider all costs when deciding if rental real estate is right for you. It's not for me.

I would have to hire someone to take care of the properties. (I am inept when it comes to working with my hands.) This would include fixing things, maintaining the property, and dealing with individuals who are having problems coming up with the rent. I don't have those issues when I invest in REITs (no calls in the middle of the night and dividends are never late). Saying all of that, there is a thing called leverage to think about.

Leverage deals with the money you borrow to buy properties (something I do not do when I buy a REIT index fund). Let's take a look at an example that might apply when buying a rental property.

- You borrow $100,000 to buy a property.
- You make a $20,000 down payment.
- The property goes up 3% in the first year.
- You make $3,000 (3% of $100,000).
- That is a 15% return ($3,000 divided by your $20,000 investment).

That sounds pretty good, right? It doesn't always work out that way. Sometimes property goes down in value or gains nothing. Leverage can be your friend and/or your enemy. Of course, the yearly expenses, which could run anywhere from 5% to 10% based on the property, are still there.

Here is another drawback when investing with one or two rental properties. You are not diversified. That REIT index fund at Vanguard has stock in over 140 real estate properties. That diversifies your risk and protects you from one or more properties performing poorly.

So what is the bottom line? If you are willing to educate yourself and buy property with a keen eye toward value and manage and maintain it yourself, you might be ready to own rental real estate. If not, join me in owning broadly diversified and inexpensive publicly traded REITs at a place like Vanguard.

"Investors who are not real estate professionals should gain exposure to the asset class through low-cost mutual funds because this is the most efficient way to achieve broad diversification."

- **Larry Swedroe,** *The Only Guide to Alternative Investments You'll Ever Need*

63

REAL ESTATE PART II

I know that last chapter was not enough to satisfy some of you on the issue. Let's continue the discussion. Investing in rental real estate really should only be done when you understand as much as possible about the location AND you are able to minimize the costs to a very low amount. Even then, I'm not sure the average person should be doing it.

I do understand why real estate is important to investors. They can touch it. They feel connected to it in ways a REIT index fund cannot do and will never do. I get that, but there are plenty of flaws beyond what I have mentioned in the previous chapter. Let's explore.

Liquidity is a big issue. How easily can you sell something so you can use the cash for your current needs? That is an important question that is answered very easily when you own a publicly-traded REIT index fund. Within 2 business days, you could sell your shares and have the money deposited in your bank account (at no cost with Vanguard REITs).

What about selling a rental property that you own in the neighborhood? That could take weeks, if not months, and there is no guarantee that you will have a buyer. You are at the mercy of that current market and location where the home is located. There are also going to be plenty of costs incurred when selling the property (a Realtor for example). Maybe a LOT of costs based on the situation.

Am I trying to talk you out of owning rental properties? Not really. I just want you to know all of the pitfalls that could come your way if you choose to go down that path. Here is the primary question I would like you to answer. Why are you investing in that rental property?

If your answer is return on investment after costs, then the REIT index fund should be the option you select in the vast majority of cases. If your answer is diversification to minimize risk, the REIT index fund stays the preferred choice. Of course, there are other things to consider.

Maybe you inherited a rental property. Maybe you like having property that isn't so easy to sell (stops you from freaking out and selling when the real estate market tanks). Maybe you got one that was severely undervalued. Maybe you bought a hunk of junk and fixed it so a family you know could live there. Maybe you like all of the tax deductions that help offset your earned income from a job.

Those are all good reasons to own rental property, and I don't blame you a bit for holding onto the property. Just be sure to track your yearly expenses when factoring in your after cost return on investment. Treat it like a real investment.

It's okay if you want to own rental property for the psychological effect. This goes back to seeing and touching something you own. It may not be the best financial decision, but it feels good. That's okay and that is your choice. Just be honest with yourself throughout the process.

Stay far away from the books, infomercials, and seminars that are pitching the no-money-down "get rich fast" real estate deals. Those people are getting rich pitching those ideas on uninformed individuals, not on investing in real estate. They are salespeople, and pretty good ones in many cases. They are trying to sell you an illusion of riches that you should avoid at all costs. Don't allow someone to get rich at your expense!

"If you want to invest in real estate without making an outsized time commitment, you can invest in REITs which are listed on the principal exchanges. They trade at prices reflecting both real estate and the overall stock market. Their long-term returns are similar to overall stock returns."

- **Charles Ellis**, *Winning the Loser's Game*

64

WHEN YOU CANNOT INDEX

There will be times for some of you when investing using index funds cannot happen. Why? There are two pretty good reasons. (1) You want to invest in an asset class that does not currently provide index funds. (2) You are stuck with a retirement plan at work that does not offer any index funds. Let's take a look at how you can deal with both issues.

Let's start with the first reason. There are asset classes that you may have difficulty finding index funds that track them. Here are two that I can see the value of owning: Treasury Inflation-Protected Securities (TIPS) and Municipal Bonds.

Both of those asset classes could be added to your portfolio (but they are certainly not required). TIPS provides you a way to protect yourself from inflation risk, and the municipal bonds provide you tax-exempt bonds that could be advantageous for many high income investors. Low- to moderate-income people should shy away from municipal bonds.

Focus on finding actively management funds that are very low cost with minimal turnover (while you wait for index funds that do it cheaper). This could easily be accomplished by requiring a yearly expense ratio below .3%. The low expense ratio happens partially due to the low turnover. You can knock out two birds with one stone by focusing on the expense ratio.

You could find both types of funds at Vanguard. Investor Shares will run you around .20% and Admiral Shares ($50,000 minimum for managed funds) will run you about .10%. Those are some really inexpensive funds that are passively invested (little turnover), but not indexed. Consider these options based on your particular situation.

Now let's look at issue number two. What happens if you have no index funds in your retirement plan? First, I would raise hell with the company (get others to raise hell with you) to get them to provide broadly diversified index funds that track the U.S. and international markets in stocks and bonds all over the world. In the meantime, focus on costs when selecting from a list of poor options.

Review all of your available investments and start weeding out the expensive ones that do not track large parts of a particular market (no sector or one asset class only funds, for example). Look for the word *total* when doing your research. This will usually mean very broad diversification over many asset class categories.

When selecting actively managed stock and bond funds, search for funds below 1% and preferably below .5%. This demonstrates low turnover most of the time by using a more passive approach. If you see expense ratios over 1% for most or all of your available options, raise hell! You deserve better choices.

If you find one or two that meet the low-cost criteria, invest with those funds until better options are made available (always consider your entire portfolio when selecting new investments). There are times in life where we have to make the best out of less than ideal situations. This could be a good example of that.

"Santa Claus and the Easter Bunny should take a few pointers from the mutual fund industry (and its fund managers). All three are trying to pull off elaborate hoaxes. But while Santa and the bunny suffer the derision of eight-year-olds everywhere, actively managed stock funds still have a ardent following among otherwise clear-thinking adults. This continued loyalty amazes me. Reams of statistics prove that most of the fund industry's stock pickers fail to beat the market."

- **Jonathon Clements**, Author of *The Little Book of Main Street Money*

65

STAY THE COURSE

Periodically, when times get rocky, you will be tempted to turn back from your journey. I have three words for you. *Stay the course*. Fear has stopped many people from reaching their goals. Folks have approached the summit only to find that monster they call fear standing in the way of reaching their dreams. *Stay the course*.

Some people fear success. Some people fear failure. Some people just fear fear! It is important to identify fear when it rises up and tries to thwart our decision-making. Fear is and always will be our enemy. This is why we must *stay the course*.

How is it that some people stick it out through thick and thin, and others turn tail and run when times get tough? While we could certainly find more than one reason, it generally comes back to a lack of faith in one's plan and one's ability to stick to that plan. This is why we need a plan. It helps us to *stay the course*.

Work your plan. A plan is what keeps a person grounded when times get tough, and there will be tough times, that we know. A plan has short-term and long-term goals that keep a person focused as they proceed forward in their investing life. It provides comfort when the roller coaster of the markets takes us for a ride. They *stay the course*.

Goals help in dealing with one or more periods of crisis, which will surely come along (life continues to throw us curve balls we never saw coming) When things don't go exactly how they are supposed to go, the plan helps a person calm their nerves as they continue down their journey. We must s*tay the course*.

When the economy or stock market falters, and it will at times, we must check our emotions at the door. Emotions sometimes lead to irrational decisions. We feel that we must do something, anything, to stop the pain. Emotions can cause us to veer away from our journey.

Don't let this happen to you. Here is a bit of news that you will rarely hear from those psychic financial media pundits: Many times the best thing to do when the markets are acting up is nothing. Stick to your plan, and when in doubt, *stay the course.*

A financial education empowers us. By learning about money, we can better understand the long history of the financial markets throughout the world. We can always refer back to times during which similar events occurred to similar people.

Markets repeat themselves over and over and over. The people who survived those times without losing their shirts, or their minds, had something in common: They pushed fear aside, stuck to their plan, checked their emotions at the door, and *stayed the course.*

You can do it!

Sometimes we all need to hear those simple words. You are capable of achieving great things, but it requires the ability to stand apart from the crowd (herd mentality). The crowd may push us to do something that is not smart. The crowd wants you to freak out as they are freaking out. You must learn to identify this folly and ignore the crowd. *Stay the course.*

"Investing is simple but not easy because, while staying the course is easy when everything is going well, when bear markets inevitably arrive, the best-laid plans can end up in the trash heap of emotions."

- **Larry Swedroe**, *The Quest for Alpha*

PUTTING

THE

P E C S

P C

I E

TOGETHER

66

BOOK SMART

Have you ever heard someone say, "He is book smart, but he has no common sense?" What do they mean by this? Usually they are referring to someone who has an education of some sort, but they don't seem to be able to apply it to real life in a common sense way. It is implied that they are educated in ways that do not translate into everyday life. Is this true, and if so, what can be done about it?

Let's face it, some people spend their life educating themselves and yet they have a hard time applying that education to life. They stumble all along the way as they try to apply what they know to their current situation. I am betting we all know one or more individuals who fit into this category. It might even be you! That does not mean that conducting research and education is a mistake. It is not. You can go back to the beginning of this book to see a good example of why research is so important.

I would like to steer this conversation toward the world of investing. We have decades and decades of research that show us how individual investors (and institutional investors) have done with investing their money.

This information has helped in creating theories that help us invest our money better so that we can capture higher returns. Modern portfolio theory (defined later in the book) was spawned based off of some of this research. So were the three-factor and five-factor models (also explained later in the book). The research provides us answers toward becoming a successful investor.

Some very smart people have taken decades of research and broken it down into small bits of information that you and I can use to become better investors. Yet many people don't. Why?

Many people would rather you listen to their personal opinions or anecdotal stories rather than focus on the facts gathered by the research. Anecdotal stories? Anyone can identify someone who "hit it big" by selecting a winning individual stock or managed mutual fund. One story should not be seen as research. It isn't.

Some people might tell you that those theories concocted by those "smart" people are nice, but they don't work in the real world and that's why you need the "helpers." That is a crock. It can be applied to real life once you fully understand how this game is played.

Here are the facts. We have an unlimited amount of evidence that shows us how to invest wisely. It's all there when we are ready to hear it, read it, and "see" it. It's time to take this to another level based on what you now know.

That research I speak of will seep out as you continue to read the following chapters. I have set the stage for you to learn about this issue of investing at a much deeper level. We are going to go in much more depth from here on out. Hang on!

"Even fans of actively managed funds often concede that most other investors would be better off in index funds. But buoyed by abundant self-confidence, these folks aren't about to give up on actively managed funds themselves. A tad delusional? I think so."

- **Paul Samuelson**, Nobel Laureate in Economics

67

BUY AND HOLD

Here is one thing we know from the research on investing. The investor who buys and holds onto an assortment of low cost index mutual funds allocated all over the world has easily outperformed the vast majority of investors over the past 90 years or so. Yet most people don't do that very simple thing. Why?

It's hard. You have all those people on Wall Street, the media, and elsewhere who are telling you to trade. They tell you to do something, don't just sit there. Here is the truth. Activity in the world of investing is a bad thing in most circumstances. Less is more and that message should resonate throughout this chapter.

The informed and successful investors will buy an assortment of index funds and strategically place them in all corners of the world in the percentage amounts that fit their risk tolerance, time horizon, goals, and other investment objectives. Once they set up the portfolio, they leave it alone to allow the markets to do what they do. They buy and then they hold. It really is that simple.

This idea of strategic asset allocation (buy many assets in the desired percentage amounts that work for you and then rebalance on occasion after that) has worked very well for the investor who is willing to apply it to their investing life. Education can enlighten AND create wealth.

The wise and successful investor ignores the daily ups and downs of the markets. As stated earlier, the informed investor also ignores the people who talk about the markets and what directions they are heading. It is irrelevant what they have to say. Ignore them.

Some "experts" want you to use tactical asset allocation (allocating your investments in an active manner toward areas in the market where you "see" inefficiencies). They tell you to move money here or there based on economical cycles and/or new developments in the world markets. This approach has failed consistently over time for the vast majority of investors. Don't do it, and don't listen to people who tell you to do it.

Buy and hold is the way to go, and the sooner the individual learns this behavior, the better their long-term returns are going to be. Yes, I said behavior. It is our daily behaviors that will either produce really good results or poor results in our portfolio over time. Buying and holding is the right behavior.

Here is one final point to ponder. Most of the time the market is going sideways (not going up or down in any significant way). There are only a few days each year where the market takes big turns on the up side. If you miss those few days, you will end up with poor returns on your portfolio as you end up sitting in cash or somewhere else "safe." You cannot afford to miss those days.

You must stay in the market to capture those limited amount of days where big returns are had. It really is all you need to know when understanding the buy and hold approach to investing. This approach has worked very well in the past and it will work in the future. Believe in that and believe in YOU.

"The American economy is going to do fine. But it won't do fine every year and every week and every month. I mean, if you don't believe that, forget about buying stocks anyway... It's a positive-sum game, long term. And the only way an investor can get killed is by high fees or by trying to outsmart the market."

- **Warren Buffett**

68

MODERN PORTFOLIO THEORY

Modern portfolio theory is a bit like fine wine. It gets better with age. Are you familiar with this thing that Harry Markowitz wrote about, way back in 1952? Let's take a trip back in time to better understand this very important theory and how to apply it to our investing life.

Mr. Markowitz theorized way back in the 1950s that you could take different securities with their own unique levels of risk, add them to a portfolio, and based on their negative correlations (asset categories that end up going in the opposite direction in relation to other asset categories), you could actually reduce the risk of the portfolio as you diversified all over the world using multiple types of these high-risk asset class categories. Bringing them all together minimized the risk as you reached for higher returns.

Think about that for a minute. You can invest using risky asset class categories like large and small U.S. stocks, international stocks, emerging markets, REITs, etc. and as you throw them together, you end up minimizing the overall risk of the portfolio.

So let's break this down even further. You look at emerging market stocks (stock in developing countries like China, India, Brazil and Russia) and you think to yourself, "those stocks are way too risky," and you are right, those types of securities are very risky.

Owning an emerging markets fund and no other stock funds would be a wild ride that could send your heart racing, but if you *added* that fund to other asset categories in a portfolio, you could reduce the risk AND keep yourself from having a heart attack. Modern portfolio theory is good for your pocketbook and your heart!

This whole thing is kind of like making a big pot of stew. Making stew with only one big jalapeno could make for a pretty hot and unpleasant experience, but if you add some potatoes, carrots, beans, meat, and maybe some spices, the stew could turn out just right. Modern portfolio theory could be seen in the same way. A proper mix of ingredients can produce a lovely portfolio that produces good returns at reasonable levels of risk.

Does modern portfolio theory offer you a risk-free option to investing? No. You could jumble up your portfolio using modern portfolio theory with a multitude of risky securities and still end up with a really bad year (see 2008 for a recent example).

This is why we add in some bonds and maybe a bit of cash into our portfolio. Back to the stew example, you would add in a few ingredients to make the stew more palatable for those who don't like spicy food. The less risky investments keep you afloat when all of the risky investments are going down, which they will do at times.

How often does everything go down at once? Not often, but it can happen, and 2008 demonstrated how many asset categories can go down at once. People who had a decent portion of bonds and cash in their portfolio (keeping 20% of your portfolio in bonds and cash is a pretty wise move even for the most aggressive investors) fared much better than the ones who had their entire portfolio in stocks. Too many jalapenos can make a stew too damn hot! Add more ingredients and your stomach AND your portfolio will benefit. Bon appetit!

"Risk and return are inextricably enmeshed. Do not expect high returns without frightening risk, and if you desire safety, you must accept low returns. The stocks of unattractive companies must, of necessity, offer higher returns than those of attractive ones; otherwise, no one would buy them. For the same reason, it is also likely that the stock returns of less developed and unstable nations are higher than those of developed nations. Anyone promising high returns with low risk is guilty of fraud."

- **William Bernstein**, *The Four Pillars of Investing*

69

THE EFFICIENT MARKET

There is a thing called the "efficient market hypothesis" that you need to know about. Here is a brief explanation of this rather mystifying subject. This hypothesis tells us that the market is efficient in the sense that all information that is known has already been factored into the share prices that make up the market (the strong version of this hypothesis includes all public information and some of those crooks who deal with inside information). Is it true?

You could find a whole lot of people who would make the case that the market is not efficient. Why would they say that? They believe they can identify where the market is inefficient and then capitalize on that weakness by buying or selling securities where they see those inefficiencies. Warren Buffett does it so they can do it! Most of these people are delusional and should be ignored.

Most people fail to capture the market inefficiencies. They talk a good game, they show up on television to tell you about it, they might even sit around the dinner table (Uncle Joe) but the truth is, most people fail to beat the market. Why? They are competing with other people (and machines that compute at amazing speeds) who have all of the same available information, and in most cases, much, much more.

When someone tries to outdo others, they are making the case that they know something someone else doesn't. Every trade requires a buyer and a seller. Most of the time that person on the other end of the trade has just as much information on securities, if not more, than you. Why would you play that loser's game? I would tell you it comes down to two things, ego and ignorance. Neither are your friends.

We should accept the reality, and the reality is whatever the market looks like today is based on all of the available information. The only thing that will change the future markets is something new that has yet to happen. **What is known is baked into the price of current markets.** It is very important for you to understand this key point.

The efficient market hypothesis does not say that the market is right all of the time. Many times it isn't. The herd pushes the market in one direction or another based on the latest bit of information or speculation. The herd overdoes it on the up side and the down side. They could be right and they could be wrong. That does not disprove this hypothesis of efficient markets. It just shows the fallibility of human beings.

Here is my advice. Accept the hypothesis, buy index funds that "own the markets," and put all of those smart people to work for you (this would include Warren Buffett as well as those crooks who use insider trading to get an unfair advantage).

That's right. By owning the markets, you have the smartest people (and the crooks) working for you every day, every month, every year, and every decade at an incredibly low cost. Winner, winner, chicken dinner!

"Markets can be highly efficient even if they make errors. Some are doozies, as when Internet stocks in the early 2000s appear to discount not only the future but the hereafter. How could it be otherwise? Stock valuations depend upon estimations of the earning power of companies many years into the future. Such forecasts are invariably incorrect. Moreover, investment risk is never clearly perceived, so the appropriate rate at which the future should be discounted is never certain. Thus, market prices must always be wrong to some extent. But at any particular time, it is not obvious to anyone whether they are too high or too low."

- **Burton Malkiel,** *A Random Walk Down Wall Street*

70

ASSET CLASSES

When investing your money, you want to own many asset classes. What is an asset class? It is securities that behave in a similar way. Let's look at four big asset classes: stocks, bonds, real estate, and cash.

In many cases, we want to own all four of these asset classes. How much per asset class? That will depend on the individual based on their goals, time horizon, risk tolerance, particular environment, and tax situation (if you are starting to see some repetition then good, it's intentional).

As I write this chapter in January 2015, owning cash makes little sense (unless you are needing it in the next few months) because of the very low interest rates. The other three assets should be owned as you break them down into pieces. Let's take a look.

When owning no-load stock index mutual funds, you would be wise to own U.S. stocks, international stocks (developed and developing countries), large companies, small companies, and value companies (see the chapter on Fama and French for the reason why).

When owning no-load bond index mutual funds, you would be wise to own U.S. bonds, international bonds, intermediate-term maturities, short-term maturities, and maybe even some inflation-protected securities (nice to have, but not required).

When owning real estate, you would be wise to own REIT's (stock in commercial real estate), and individual rental properties (not required). Your personal home is not an investment as we have already covered. Buy a home to live in for pleasure only.

You can own all of those asset class categories at a very low cost in those no-load index mutual funds. I'm sure you have noticed how many times I have referenced no-load index mutual funds. I am hoping to stamp that term forever into your brain. Owning multiple types of asset class categories is good. Owning them at the lowest possible cost is great. No-load index mutual funds will do that.

You don't need to own a lot of index funds to be diversified all over the world. I personally own eight index funds. You could own three and beat the vast majority of investors. Here they are:

(1) A **total stock market index fund** that owns the U.S. economy.
(2) A **total international stock index fund** that owns much of the developed and developing companies overseas.
(3) A **total bond market index fund** that owns a large swath of quality government and corporate bonds in the U.S.A.

Do not overlap your funds. All this means is you don't own two funds that do the same thing. You don't own two total stock market funds or two total international funds that own developed countries. One is all you need per allocation.

This chapter should help you in adding to what you know about asset allocation and modern portfolio theory. Does it seem complicated? It really isn't. It just takes a bit of time and education and gradually you will get it. Keep reading and keep learning. Knowledge is POWER. Follow that knowledge with action and you can change your life!

"At its core, asset allocation is a strategy of risk diversification; different asset classes and categories have different risks that are not related to one another. Holding fundamentally different investments in a portfolio, each with an expected real return over inflation, reduces overall portfolio risk and increases return in the long run."

- **Rick Ferri,** *All About Asset Allocation*

71

NEGATIVE CORRELATIONS

You want to build your portfolio with negatively correlated assets. Informed investors know this, but it is easier said than done. So what is a negatively correlated asset? Think of it in relation to when you were a child playing on the seesaw (also known as the teeter-totter). When one side goes up, the other goes down and vice versa. You don't go up together and you don't go down together.

Negatively correlated assets tend to go up or down in opposite directions. You might ask why is it important to have negatively correlated assets? You don't want everything in your portfolio to go down at the same time! Yes, it would be wonderful if everything went up at the same time, but that's stretching reality a bit too far. We want different assets in our portfolio to run counter to each other so the downturns are not so bad.

I hope all of that made sense. Now I am going to talk about the difficulties of doing it. The negative correlation between assets is fluid and changing all of the time. This simply means you must be aware that the correlations between assets can and will change over time. Sometimes they change only slightly and sometimes they can change quite a lot. With that caveat, let's take a look at how to construct a portfolio as best we can using a multitude of assets that do have some degree of negative correlation.

Here are some basics. Stocks tend to run in a different direction than bonds. U.S. stocks tend to run a different direction than international stocks (the range has reduced over the years due to globalization). Large stocks run in a different direction than small stocks (include REITs with small stocks). Growth stocks run different than value stocks. It can get more complex, but these are good places to start.

Now let's see how to construct a portfolio in the real world using this concept of negative correlations. You have a 401(k) at work. You have a Roth IRA at Vanguard. You have a traditional IRA at Vanguard that you moved there from an old employer's 401(k) plan years ago. Finally, you have two non-retirement accounts at Vanguard that you access when needed for emergencies and future plans prior to retirement.

You could own a total stock market index fund in your non-retirement stock fund (very tax efficient), and a short-term bond index fund for your emergencies. You could own a total international index fund and an emerging markets stock index fund in your current 401(k). You could own a small-cap value index fund and a large cap value index fund in your traditional IRA. Finally, you could own a REIT index fund, a total international bond index fund (not required), and a total bond market index fund in your Roth IRA. Voila!

What about percentages? It is not a perfect science regarding how much to have in one fund vs. another. As a good rule of thumb, you want to have the biggest chunk of your money in the broadly diversified funds that own entire markets. This would include a total U.S. market index fund and a total international market index fund when it comes to stocks and a U.S. total bond market index fund in regard to owning bonds.

Educate yourself carefully prior to allocating those negatively correlated assets within your portfolio and then monitor them over time, rebalancing when needed. Success will follow.

"Investors can avoid timing problems—when to change from one market and its index to another—and almost all taxes by the simplest strategy: holding on for the very long term. Of course, this depends on selecting the right index fund at the beginning. That's why wise investors choose an index fund that replicates the broadest market. For fairly rational investors, this will be a broad market index fund in their own country. For very rational investors, this will be a worldwide total market index fund."

- **Charles Ellis**, *Winning the Loser's Game*

Stock and Bond Market Returns

The data was retrieved from the S&P 500 Dow Jones Indices and the Federal Reserve Data Base. Reinvested yearly dividends and interest are included in the total returns (before costs). Losing years are highlighted. Notice how often one asset is going down when the other asset is going up. This is what negative correlation looks like.

Year	S&P 500 Index	10 Year Bond Index
1992	7.62%	9.36%
1993	10.08%	14.21%
1994	1.32%	-8.04%
1995	37.58%	23.48%
1996	22.96%	1.43%
1997	33.36%	9.94%
1998	28.58%	14.92%
1999	21.04%	-8.25%
2000	-9.10%	16.66%
2001	-11.89%	5.57%
2002	-22.10%	15.12%
2003	28.68%	.38%
2004	10.88%	4.49%
2005	4.91%	2.87%
2006	15.79%	1.96%
2007	5.49%	10.21%
2008	-37.00%	20.10%
2009	26.46%	-11.12%
2010	15.06%	8.46%
2011	2.11%	16.04%
2012	16.00%	2.97%
2013	32.39%	-9.10%
2014	13.69%	10.75%
2015	???????	???????

72

HOW MUCH IN STOCKS?

How much should you own in stocks in relation to your entire portfolio? It depends. It depends because each situation is different and each human being is different. Know thyself before making this very important decision.

This goes back to answering some big questions. What is your time horizon (how long before you need the money)? What is your risk tolerance (at what point would you freak out and sell based on a big drop in the markets)? What are your goals (retirement, college, escape from work, etc.)? What is your tax situation (do you find yourself in a high tax bracket or low tax bracket)? Here is one final question: Do you need income from your investments to cover some or all of your monthly expenses?

It is important to answer all of these questions as you settle into your decision on how much stock to own in your portfolio. It really is a personal decision and only you can make it based on your own unique situation. Here are three mighty smart men with their recommendations. Identify where you fall as you review their advice.

- **Conservative investor** (John Bogle): Have your age in bonds and cash. Keep the rest in stocks.

- **Moderately aggressive investor** (Burton Malkiel): Keep an extra 10% to 20% extra in stocks beyond the conservative approach.

- **Aggressive investor** (Charles Ellis): Keep an extra 10% to 20% extra in stocks beyond the moderately aggressive approach.

Now let's look at a real-life situation. We have a 40-year-old woman by the name of Cynthia. She is educated on the world of investing and now she needs to decide how much she will allocate to stocks. She asks herself all of the important questions and then she considers her options.

- **Conservative investor:** 60% in stocks / 40% in bonds

- **Moderately aggressive investor:** 70% in stocks / 30% in bonds

- **Aggressive investor:** 80% in stocks / 20% in bonds

In this case Cynthia decides she belongs in the moderate category so she will break her portfolio down into 70% stocks and 30% bonds. This may change over time as Cynthia's situation changes (including her age), but for right now, this is right for Cynthia.

You can go through the same process. Take your time to grasp some of the nuances that come with this issue. How much should you own in U.S. vs. international stocks and bonds? How much emphasis do you place on REITs in your portfolio? Are you going to overweight toward value and small stocks? How much are you saving each month and how is that affecting your asset allocation?

As you can see, this issue gets more complicated as you dig deeper into the matter. That's okay. Take it one step at a time as you chart a course for your future. You can do it and you should do it if you want financial freedom to enter your life.

"Unless you still believe in the tooth fairy, you will want to select an index fund for every asset category. The advantages are compelling. ... Do the right thing: In every asset class where they are available, index!"

- **Frank Armstrong III**, *The Informed Investor*

73

FAMA AND FRENCH

The informed investor knows who Eugene Fama and Kenneth French are and what they have provided to the investment community. These two men identified through extensive research that there were three factors (the three-factor model) that could account for almost all of the return in a diversified equity portfolio. Those three factors were the market, size, and the book/market ratio. Let's explore the issue.

Here is what they found. Looking at the broad market returns could only tell you part of the story when looking at the returns of a particular portfolio. You also needed to look at size (how many large companies were held vs. small companies) and book/market ratio (how many value companies were held vs. growth companies). When you took all that into account, it told you just about everything you needed to know about the returns on the equity (stock) portion of the portfolio.

This empirical data was telling us something very important. Over the last 80+ years, a portfolio that had more small and value companies had remarkably higher returns. In any given year that could change, but over many years, it benefitted the investor to overweight (have more of) their portfolio by owning more small companies and value companies.

So how does a person apply this in real life? You can own a total stock market index fund. That is the market. You can own a value index fund. That will overweight you to large value stocks. You can own a small-cap value index fund. That will overweight you toward small companies and value companies all in one fund. Voila. You have now overweighted your portfolio toward small and value companies. Congratulations!

Why would you not do this? There are a couple of reasons. (1) It will be slightly more expensive. (2) The past is not the future. It is a guarantee that the future will be different from the past. How different, and in what ways, nobody really knows.

Do I overweight my portfolio toward small and value companies? I sure do, and I have been doing it for well over a decade. Should you? That's your call. Educate yourself on the matter, review the empirical evidence and then you decide whether or not to overweight your portfolio toward those small and value companies.

We're not quite done with what we have learned from Fama and French. There are two more factors to consider on the bond side of things. They are quality and term (this is described as the five-factor model). The quality deals with highly rated bonds (belonging to strong companies) and the term deals with the length of the maturities of the bonds.

The idea is to own only quality bonds (no junk bonds) and only short- to intermediate-term bonds (keep the maturities under 10 years and preferably closer to 5).

How do you apply this in real life? Stick with a total bond market index fund and/or a total international bond index fund (intermediate maturities) and/or a short-term bond index fund (maturities that run closer to 2 or 3 years). The empirical data demonstrates this to be a wise move. Educate and ACT.

"Indexing is a marvelous technique. I wasn't a true believer. I was just an ignoramus. Now I am a convert. Indexing is an extraordinary sophisticated thing to do… If people want excitement, they should go to the racetrack or play the lottery."

> - **Douglas Dial**, Former Manager of the CREF Stock Account

74

BREAKING IT DOWN

This chapter is designed to help you understand how to break down your portfolio into the desired allocations that fit your present and future needs. It will build off the chapter on asset allocation. The differences are small, but important.

You will see my desired asset allocation numbers below (100% is in index funds). I advise you to take my numbers and use them as an example to create your numbers. **I am not saying these should be your numbers.** That is something you need to figure out. Let's take a look at my numbers.

- **My age:** 51

- **My stock allocation:** 80%

- **My bond allocation:** 20%

- **My stock breakdown:** 70% U.S. and 30% international

- **My bond breakdown:** 80% U.S. and 20% international

- **My bond breakdown by quality:** 100% high quality (no junk)

- **My U.S. stock breakdown:** 70% Total Stock, 10% REITs, 10% small value, and 10% large value

- **My international stock breakdown:** 70% developed countries and 30% emerging markets (developing countries)

How does this look in real numbers? The breakdown is stated below. I have chosen a portfolio of **$100,000** for this example. Always identify your total amount prior to allocating assets. You will need to add up all of your money in all accounts to see what that number is for you.

- **My stock allocation:** $80,000

- **My bond allocation:** $20,000

- **My stock breakdown:** $56,000 U.S. and $24,000 international

- **My bond breakdown:** $16,000 U.S. and $4,000 international

- **My bond breakdown by quality:** $20,000 high quality (no junk)

- **My U.S. stock breakdown:** $39,200 Total Stock, $5,600 REITs, $5,600 small value, and $5,600 large value

- **My international stock breakdown:** $16,800 developed countries and $7,200 emerging markets

That is how I break down my investments based on my desired asset allocation. You can do the same with a bit of education as you identify your desired numbers and the total amount of money you have to work with. My entire portfolio cost is .10%. Strive to get your number down to that level or lower. Higher returns will follow!

"There is one investment truism that, if followed, can dependably increase your investment returns: Minimize your investment costs."

- **Burton Malkiel and Charles Ellis**, *The Elements of Investing*

75

IN ANY GIVEN YEAR...

In any given year any asset class can drop in value. That does not make that particular asset class or category a bad investment. It simply demonstrates how the markets work. You can select any year from the past and see what were the best investments to own during that year and what were the worst. It's easy to do AFTER it has happened. It is impossible to do BEFORE the coming year. This is why diversification is so important.

Let's take a look. In 2014, the U.S. stock market (we will use the S&P 500 for this example) did quite well. It earned 13.69%. The overseas market (we will use an index that tracks developed countries like Canada, Germany, England, and France) produced a return of -9.32%. So the U.S. market made over 24% more than the international market. I should have had all of my investments in the U.S. stock market, right? Wrong! The returns could have been reversed.

Every year you and I will wish we had more money in the winning asset classes and less money in the losing asset classes. The problem here is nobody knew that was going to happen. And when I say nobody, I mean *nobody*. This is why we diversify our investments all over the world in multiple types of asset classes. Diversification saves our portfolio from taking very big drops as we avoid putting all of our eggs in one basket.

This chapter runs parallel with the chapter on modern portfolio theory. It is critical that we place many different asset classes in our portfolio as we strive to garner the market returns at the lowest possible cost AND at the lowest risk. This does not mean we can avoid asset class categories that lose value in any given year. That comes with the territory and the informed investor knows that.

So what are you to do when you have an asset class that lost money in the previous year? Buy more of it! Of course, all I am really saying is you should rebalance your portfolio to get your percentages back to where you want them to be. You buy your losers and sell your winners.

This is very rational and very smart, but not so easy to do. Another way to deal with this situation is to simply put more new money into the funds that have performed poorly. Dollar-cost averaging (select a set amount and invest it every month) money into the past year's losers can be an effective and simple way to handle this situation.

So what are some of the big takeaways from this chapter? It is normal and expected to have asset classes and categories in your portfolio go down in any given year. That's how it works.

You haven't done anything wrong. You placed negatively correlated asset categories in your portfolio knowing that in any given year; some will not perform as well as others. That's why you placed negatively correlated assets in the portfolio!

You know how this all works and you accept the reality of the situation even though you don't like the fact that you owned losing investments. You have come to realize it's the return on the portfolio that matters, not the individual investments within the portfolio. You have become the informed and successful investor.

"No matter how you allocate your assets, you will always wish that you had assigned more to the best performer and nothing at all to the worst performer. Since no one can predict which these will be, the safest course is to own them all, and thereby, as best you can, assure yourself of not being devastated by an Enron or a Lehman. When you minimize your expenses and diversify, you forego bragging rights with the neighbors and in-laws, but you will also minimize the chances of impoverishing yourself and the ones you love."

- **William Bernstein,** *The Investor's Manifesto*

76

THE SECTOR FUND

Many years ago, the investing world got a lot more complicated when sector funds were created and marketed to the average investor. A sector fund invests in a very specific part of the economy. You might see a sector fund that owns gold mining companies, energy companies, health care companies, or maybe even technology companies. Should you own these types of investments?

In most cases, the answer is no. Why? When selecting a specific sector, you are basically attempting to predict the future by focusing on certain sectors over others. You are choosing to overweight your portfolio toward those particular sectors, which by the way, you would already own in a broadly diversified fund like the Total Stock Market Index Fund at Vanguard. It's not wise to think you know something others don't (in case you are wondering, overweighting to small and value via Fama and French is a totally different concept based on previous results).

Is there an exception? Yes, I believe there is. I would recommend you consider owning a REIT index fund (stock in commercial real estate like hotels, office buildings, and malls). Why? A total stock market index fund will own REITs, but not in the same amount that is reflected in the actual U.S. economy. If you do not own a REIT fund, you will not have a portfolio that reflects the true economy of the United States.

What did I just say? If you want to own the real U.S. economy, you will have to add a REIT index fund to your portfolio to do that. This type of fund belongs in your small company category and it tends to be negatively correlated to many other types of assets. It can provide a nice addition to a portfolio to broaden the diversification even further.

This sector fund provides a great deal of yearly income (dividends), so it is wise to keep it in a retirement account at work or in a Roth IRA outside of work. It is not a tax efficient fund (see the chapter on taxes for a better understanding on tax efficiency).

How much? There is no perfect allocation percentage for this investment. My recommendation is to keep about 10% of your U.S. stock allocation in REITs. Note that I said 10% of your U.S. stock allocation, not 10% of your entire portfolio. You don't want to get too far away from the market and that means not an exaggerated overweighting of REITs within your portfolio.

Be careful! Many brokers will try to sell you private REITs that lock up your money for long periods of time. These are not the same as the publicly traded REITs I just mentioned. The broker gets a big fat commission and you get something you don't understand and can't access when you want it. Avoid these poor types of investments. It will be easy to do if you avoid all brokers, which you should.

Let's wrap this up. Sector funds should be avoided in most cases for most people with the exception of the REIT index fund. Trying to predict the future of certain sectors in the economy can be an expensive mistake. If you are doing it, stop. If you are contemplating it, don't.

"Investors, both individual and institutional, and particularly 401(k) plans, would be far better served by investing in passive or passively managed funds than in trying to pick more expensive active managers who purport to be able to beat the markets."

- **Edward S. O'Neal Ph.D.**, after completing a study of 494 actively managed mutual funds that attempted to beat the S&P 500 index for the period July 1993 through June 2003, 98% failed to do it, 10 funds (2%) succeeded.

77

HOW MANY FUNDS?

How many no-load index mutual funds should you own? Here is another answer you may not like. It depends. This is a pretty tricky question and the answer I give you may not make much sense. Sorry about that, but there are many nuances that come with this issue.

You could own two Vanguard funds and beat the vast majority of investors. Yes, two! You could own the **Total Stock Market Index Fund Admiral Shares** (.05% expense ratio) and the **Total Bond Market Index Fund Admiral Shares** (.07% expense ratio) in the allocations that are right for you based on your time horizon, risk tolerance and other considerations. If you want to add more diversification, keep reading.

You could the Vanguard **Total International Stock Index Fund Admiral Shares** (.14% expense ratio) for further diversification and possibly higher returns.

If you like, you could add other index funds from Vanguard to further diversify you all over the world. You could add the **Emerging Markets Stock Index Fund Admiral Shares** (.15% expense ratio) and/or you could add the **REIT Index Fund Admiral Shares** (.10% expense ratio) per the last chapter.

You could add the **Value Index Fund Admiral Shares** (.09% expense ratio) and the **Small-Cap Value Index Fund Admiral Shares** (.09% expense ratio) to add a piece to your portfolio that uses the research from Fama and French to help you overweight toward value and small company stocks. Do you have to add these funds? No, and you may not want to, but you certainly might consider it.

You might consider the **Total Bond International Index Fund Admiral Shares** (.19% expense ratio). That bond fund is not required, but it is certainly worth considering. Could you add others? Sure, but keep in mind, the more you overweight your portfolio away from the global market, the more likely you are going to experience tracking error (you fail to capture the market returns because of your overweighting elsewhere).

When you add all of those other funds to a portfolio, you add more moving parts that you hope will add value to your return AND reduce the risk of your portfolio. It might work and it might not. Does that sound wishy-washy? It probably does, but there lies our dilemma as investors. How many funds an investor should own is not a perfect science no matter how hard we try to make it one.

What do I do? I own index funds beyond just the U.S. stock and bond markets. I own international stock and bond funds. I own REITs. I own value and small company funds. Does that mean I will outperform someone who owns the Total Stock Market Index Fund and Total Bond Market Index Fund only? Nope.

It just means I believe in modern portfolio theory, and I believe the research from Fama and French will continue to demonstrate a benefit toward overweighting a portfolio toward value and small company stock.

This is where you must make a decision. Educate yourself and don't get too cute. Own total stock and bond market index funds and add a little extra if you are so inclined. Make the call!

"A minuscule 4 percent of funds produce market-beating after-tax results with a scant 0.6 percent (annual) margin of gain. The 96 percent of funds that fail to meet or beat the Vanguard 500 Index Fund lose by a wealth-destroying margin of 4.8 percent per annum."

- **David Swensen**, Chief Investment Officer at Yale University

78

REBALANCING

Rebalancing your portfolio is a good idea, but hard to do for many. Why? When you rebalance, you are selling your winners and buying your losers. Do you want to do that? Most people don't. We like our winning investments and we complain about our losing investments. Buying more of the losers and selling the winners is counterintuitive and yet, that is exactly what you should do when rebalancing. Let's explore further.

Over any given time period you will have certain asset classes in your portfolio that will do well and certain asset classes that won't. That is reality. The informed investor owns the world in stocks and bonds and accepts the ups and downs of each market.

So when your portfolio gets out of whack (some markets have gone up while others have gone down), you buy more stocks (or bonds). You simply want to get back to the desired asset allocation that is right for you.

As discussed earlier, if you prefer a 70% stock allocation and 30% bond allocation and your portfolio is now at 82% stocks and 18% bonds, you will want to sell some stocks and buy some bonds so you end up back at your desired asset allocation of 70% stocks and 30% bonds.

What I just stated is very rational, but we also know human beings are not always so rational. Emotions bubble up and that can play a much bigger part in our decision-making. So will you be rational or emotional on this decision? Let me restate that question. Will you rebalance to reduce your risk and possibly increase your return over time or will you avoid it and take on more risk and receive possibly lower returns? I think we know what the right thing is to do.

How often should you rebalance? That is a more difficult question. There is no research that I am aware of that demonstrates a benefit to doing it more than once per year. Personally, I don't rebalance until my percentage of stocks or bonds go beyond 10% of my desired stock or bond allocations. If my desired amount of stocks is 80%, I won't make any changes to the portfolio until it drops below 70% or goes above 90%. This usually causes me to rebalance once every few years.

Here is another option. You might decide to go into your portfolio one time each year and rebalance your portfolio back to your desired allocations no matter how little they are out of whack. That is just fine and there is nothing wrong with that approach. The key is to select one approach and then stick to it over time.

What stocks to buy or sell? This is pretty easy. Buy or sell the ones that have gone down or up the most. This will bring you in line with your desired allocations with all of your asset class categories within your portfolio. Don't complicate this. Sell the big winners and buy the big losers.

When rebalancing, do it in tax-sheltered accounts like your 401(k) or a Roth IRA to avoid tax consequences. You can also add or withdraw money from taxable accounts and retirement accounts to accomplish the same rebalancing effect. Get a plan and stick to it. Lower risk will follow.

This chapter might be pretty confusing to many. Rebalancing is a new concept that takes a bit of time to understand and apply to your portfolio, but it is well worth your time and effort. Stay rational in this very irrational world. Lower risk and higher returns will usually follow.

"Portfolio rebalancing is a fundamental part of asset allocation. Rebalancing reduces portfolio risk and creates a diversification benefit in the form of a higher long-term return."

- **Rick Ferri**, *All About Asset Allocation*

79

ASSET ALLOCATION

Now we can start using what we know to identify our desired allocations. How you deal with the asset allocation of your investments will play the biggest impact on your portfolio return over time.

What is your time horizon? What are your goals? How much risk can you handle? What is your tax situation? Do you need income from your investments? Below you will see a list of questions I have posed to you earlier. Now it is your turn to answer them. Write your answers down beside the questions.

- **What is your desired allocation?**

- **How would you like your stocks broken down?**

- **How would you like to break down U.S. stocks?**

- **How would you like to break down international stocks?**

- **How would you like your bonds broken down?**

- **When will you rebalance?**

This will get you moving in the right direction. Are you married? Be sure to include your spouse in the conversation. Do you deal with your portfolio separately or do you combine portfolios with him or her? That needs to be answered as well. Try to make these very important decisions with as much available information as possible. This is your future! Next up, buying the investments.

This is actually quite simple. Buy no-load index mutual funds whenever possible as you allocate investments within your portfolio. You can identify different funds based on what they invest in by reviewing their prospectus provided by the investment company. Then you buy them in the percentages that you have identified as being the right assets to own based on your particular situation.

Index funds should be purchased with a close eye toward their costs. NEVER pay a load. NEVER pay an expense ratio beyond .5% (although you may not have a choice based on availability in retirement accounts). Strive to get your portfolio expense ratio down to .10%. This will assist you in keeping most of your final return as you distance yourself from the "helpers" and the expensive products they sell.

This chapter should help you further in "connecting the dots." This issue of asset allocation becomes much more understandable as your level of knowledge on the issue of investing rises. Read this chapter again if necessary. Financial freedom will come to those who see the truth. That can be you. Onward!

"We invest with faith in the financial markets, dividing our portfolios among distinct asset classes that blossom and wither in different seasons of the economic cycle. Following the simple logic of diversification, we seek to maximize our participation in the market's seasons of plenty, while ensuring that we survive it in seasons of want."

- **John Bogle,** *Common Sense on Mutual Funds*

Asset Allocation by the Numbers

These numbers were retrieved from vanguard.com and deal with the historical returns based on a portfolio divided up between stocks and bonds. The time period runs from 1926 to 2013.

Note: This time period includes the Great Depression and the lousy stock returns of the first decade of the 21st century. Use these historical averages as a guide, not a prediction when you are identifying the right asset allocation for you.

Asset Allocation Options	Historic Average
100% Bonds	5.5%
80% Bonds / 20% Stocks	6.7%
70% Bonds / 30% Stocks	7.4%
60% Bonds / 40% Stocks	7.8%
50% Bonds / 50% Stocks	8.3%
40% Bonds / 60% Stocks	8.9%
30% Bonds / 70% Stocks	9.2%
20% Bonds / 80% Stocks	9.6%
100% Stocks	10.2%

80

ALL IN ONE

There is a type of mutual fund that attempts to diversify you all over the world and rebalance consistently over time without any effort on your part. Basically, you own the world in one fund. That sounds pretty good, right? It can be, but it requires a bit of education first.

There are many names that go with these types of all-in-one funds. Here are four: lifecycle, asset allocation, lifestrategy and target date retirement. These funds are similar, but not the same. They own multiple asset classes in one fund as they diversify you over all parts of the world in stocks and bonds. Of course, there is more to it than that.

Some of these funds have a number attached to them like 2020 or 2050, for example. You can use these numbers to select a fund that fits your time horizon. For example, if you plan on retiring some time around the year 2020, you might consider selecting a fund with the year 2020 attached to it. If there is no number the allocations generally stay static over time. This simply means your allocations don't change.

Over time, the target date retirement funds that have numbers will become more conservative (own more bonds and less stock). When you land on the year you have selected, the fund may continue to become more conservative or it may keep your investments static. The prospectus for the fund will explain each fund's particular approach when investing.

Are they all the same? No, and that is an understatement. Many all-in-one funds use actively managed funds, instead of index funds (avoid the actively managed funds). They all use slightly different asset allocation models. Finally, they all have different costs associated with each fund.

So, what criteria should you use when selecting one of these types of investments? (1) You want an all index approach. (2) You want the expense ratio below .2%. Get those two things accomplished and you will be ready to select a fund that fits your particular situation.

Where? Vanguard should be your default in most cases. Vanguard's target date retirement funds charge anywhere from .16% to .18% per year. They are made up of Vanguard index funds. To be specific they own primarily these four funds:

- **Total Stock Market Index Fund**
- **Total International Stock Index Fund**
- **Total Bond Market Index Fund**
- **Total International Bond Index Fund**

So is this a better option than owning individual index funds at Vanguard? It depends. It will cost you slightly more than an all index approach with Admiral Shares ($10,000 minimum investment), but it could cost you less than an all-index approach with Investor Shares ($3,000 minimum investment). They also have a very inexpensive initial investment minimum of $1,000. It is certainly worth considering.

So should you do it? If you like the simplicity of owning just one fund that rebalances on its own, this might be a very good option. If you prefer to handle the rebalancing yourself and can afford Admiral Shares, you might consider owning the individual index funds. Both options are good and very inexpensive when done at Vanguard. Take your time and think about your choices before deciding. Pick the one that fits you and your investing style and move on.

"Indeed, you can look at any meaningful time period and you will find that the majority of hyperactively managed funds fail to beat an unmanaged S&P 500 index, even when it is their stated goal to do so."

- **Daniel Solin**, *The Smartest Investment Book You'll Ever Read*

81

SUCCESS!

How do you define success when it comes to investing? Here is how some people do it. They brag about some winning stock (Uncle Joe) or mutual fund, or alternative investment to their buddies. Is that success when someone picks something out of the blue to brag about?

Of course not, it is simply one investment that went well (at least according to the person who is doing the bragging based on one specific time period). *That is anecdotal.* One positive experience does not equal skill. Always be on the lookout for anecdotal explanations being spewed out by the uninformed investor or the salesperson who is calling an event after it has occurred (see the "data mining" definition in the glossary). The question still remains: "How should we define success when investing?"

The answer is: How close did you get to capturing the market returns? That's it. How close did you get to matching the market returns during any time period you choose based on the markets you were investing in within your portfolio? Is that complicated? No, but it may take a bit more explaining. Let's take a look.

You have selected an 80% stock and 20% bond allocation based on your particular situation (you answered all those questions on risk tolerance, time horizon, goals, and taxes prior to making that decision). You are an informed investor, so you went straight to index funds. You focused on an all index portfolio and because of that, your costs were reduced to .08% for your entire portfolio. So far; so good I would say.

The markets (stock and bond markets all over the world) ended up producing a minuscule return of 1% for the year. After subtracting .08% in yearly fees, you are left with a return of .92%. Well done!

Now I know some of you are not going to be impressed with that minimal return, but that is how you should gauge success. By capturing market returns as closely as possible year after year, you will end up becoming a very successful investor.

The markets will beat most investors on a yearly basis and almost all investors over periods of time that span decades. Every year you capture something close to market returns is a year that moves you toward becoming the highly successful investor.

This means you will outperform the vast majority of investors all over the world. That is success, and the sooner in life you learn that, the better off you are going to be as an investor.

Whether you capture a .92% return or a 32% return, you are successful when those returns track market returns minus a very small fee that you pay to own index funds that track markets all over the world.

Please take the time to reread this chapter. It will help guide you toward becoming that informed, wise, efficient, and successful investor. By understanding how we define success, we are well on our way toward achieving it.

"You are engaged in a life-and-death struggle with the financial services industry. Every dollar in fees, expenses, and spreads you pay them comes directly out of your pocket. If you act on the assumption that every broker, insurance salesman, mutual fund salesperson, and financial advisor you encounter is a hardened criminal, you will do just fine."

- **William Bernstein,** *The Investor's Manifesto*

82

THE KNOWLEDGEABLE INVESTOR

Knowledgeable investors become successful investors as they apply what they learn about the industry and the products they sell. Let's recap what we have learned and what direction we should go when investing our savings for our future needs.

- Select your asset allocation, and then rebalance every year or so. Consider having your bond/cash allocation equaling something close to your age. One size does not fit all, though. The key is to identify what is right for you and then stick to it.

- Buy the most inexpensive no-load index mutual funds that are offered. Go to vanguard.com when possible and focus on the index funds that diversify you over large sectors of the US and international economies in stocks and bonds.

- Own at least one total stock market index fund and at least one short- or intermediate-term bond index fund. You can easily buy one target date retirement fund that does all of this for you.

- Stay away from commission-based brokers and advisors. You don't need them and you certainly cannot afford them.

- As your portfolio grows, consider diversifying your portfolio further with an international stock index fund, an emerging stock index fund, a small-cap value index fund, a large-cap value index fund, and a REIT index fund. Once again, one or more target date retirement funds will suffice.

- Disregard people who tell you there are better ways to invest your hard earned money. Becoming one of the top 20 percent of investors in the world is good enough.

- Check your funds infrequently. Once a year is perfectly acceptable. Be an investor not a speculator and that means ignoring most of what you hear and see coming from media sources.

- Laugh at the day-to-day hyperbole that you see on television, the Internet, and magazines. Human beings cannot predict the future, but they continue to try.

- Take your emotions out of your investing decisions. This is done with education and the ability to stick to a written down plan that contains your goals. Know thyself.

- If you need a thrill, go climb a mountain. Don't try to find it in your investments. Investing should be boring.

- If you need help, reach out to a fee-only advisor/planner (keep reading) who will guide you without the rampant conflicts of interest that dominate the financial services industry.

- Stay the course. Buy and hold your investments, and just ignore the market-timing experts who are wrong more times than they are right. You are the wise and successful investor.

"The S&P is up 343.8 percent for 10 years. That is a four-bagger. The general equity funds are up 283 percent. So it's getting worse, the deterioration by professionals is getting worse. The public would be better off in an index fund."

- **Peter Lynch**, One of the most successful mutual fund managers (Magellan Fund at Fidelity) of all time

Stage V

FINAL

THOUGHTS

83

CONTINUOUS LEARNING

I would like you to see this as the beginning of your learning when it comes to investing and all of the forces working against you. Whether you are a beginner, intermediate or advanced person when it comes to investing, there is always plenty to learn on the subject. Never stop being a student. Keep stretching yourself!

I have tried to expose you to many independent sources who have plenty to share with you on becoming the wise and successful investor. I would strongly encourage you to pick up some of their books and continue your education far beyond what you have read here.

This book is simply a condensed version of hundreds of other books on investing that I have read over the years. I learn and I share. You can do the same with your circle of friends, family and acquaintances. Do not underestimate how big of an impact a book can have on your life.

Where do you start? This can be a bit tricky because we are all at different points along the continuum of investing knowledge. Think of it as a scale ranging from 0 to 10. Where are you at this time on that scale?

Think of a beginner at 3 or less. An intermediate might fall between 3 and 7. Finally, advanced investors might be anyone above 7. Once you identify your current number (it is always changing), pick up a book from the recommended list that follows.

Here are my recommendations for the beginner, intermediate or advanced person. Strive to learn more and more as you proceed further along on that continuum. It can and will change your life!

Beginner

- *The Little Book of Common Sense Investing* by John Bogle
- *The Smartest Investment Book You'll Ever Read* by Daniel Solin
- *The Elements of Investing* by Charles Ellis and Burton Malkiel

Intermediate

- *Winning the Loser's Game* by Charles Ellis
- *The Informed Investor* by Frank Armstrong III
- *A Random Walk Down Wall Street* by Burton Malkiel

Advanced

- *The Four Pillars of Investing* by William Bernstein
- *Common Sense on Mutual Funds* by John Bogle
- *Unconventional Success* by David Swensen

There are a great many nuances that come with investing. As you start to expand your knowledge on this subject, you will realize just how much you did not know. That's okay. People who have become informed on this subject have gone through the same transformation. Keep learning. Keep growing and keep changing. Financial freedom is waiting for you!

"Mutual funds are run by highly experienced and hard working professionals who buy and sell stocks to achieve the best possible results for their clients. Nevertheless, the evidence from more than fifty years of research is conclusive: for a large majority of fund managers, the selection of stocks is more like rolling dice than like playing poker."

- **Daniel Kauneman**, Nobel Laureate in Economics

84

THE FEE-ONLY ADVISOR

If you need help with your investments beyond what you can do for yourself, go to napfa.org and identify a fee-only financial advisor near you. You can type in your zip code to identify an advisor close to home. Why do this? You want to identify a true professional who will guide you without the inherent conflicts of interest that are widespread in the financial services industry. **Fee-only trumps fee-based** on this very important issue.

Why would I recommend a fee-only advisor when I say you can do this yourself? I know some of you won't and others simply can't. I also know many of you may need help when it comes to the psychological part of the investing game. You can do everything right, but if you freak out and sell when the market drops, you can end up destroying all of the good you have done. This is why it is important to get help if you need it.

You want to find an advisor who works for you and only you. You pay them for their services. You get a bill (if you don't get a bill, you're most likely working with the wrong people). They work as a true fiduciary when making recommendations and investing your money. They have a legal duty to act solely in your best interests. That is a big deal and that is the only person you want when seeking assistance.

A stockbroker as stated earlier, is not a fiduciary. What about a fee-*based* advisor? By law they are, the conflicts of interest tell us a different story. When it looks like a pig, smells like a pig, and sounds like a pig, it's a pig! This is why we identify a fee-*only* advisor when seeking a true fiduciary. That does not mean the job is done, though. There are a few obstacles to overcome as we seek out the "right" fee-only advisor.

Most fee-only financial advisors have dollar minimums. $250,000 tends to be the lowest amount needed before they take you on as a client. Some fee-only advisors are starting to drop that number to $100,000 or less. Take a look at Garrett Financial Planning. They offer hourly-based services with no minimums. That can work for many investors. Learn more here: (garrettplanningnetwork.com).

You can reach out to one of the new Robo Advisors (like Betterment.com). They charge .35% or less. Try to keep your total expenses (what you pay the advisor plus what you pay for your investments) below .50%. An all-index portfolio should do the trick. Vanguard provides a similar service at a fee of .30%.

Not all fee-only advisors are the same. You need to identify the true experts on the subject prior to giving them your money. **Some fee-only advisors should be avoided**. What would you ask a fee-only financial advisor when considering using their services? Here is a short list. The answers you would want to hear follow the questions.

- How much do you charge? **1% or less**
- Do you try to time the market? **No**
- Do you try to predict what markets are going up or down? **No**
- Do you invest passively using index funds and ETFs? **Yes**

If you did not get those answers, go find someone else. There is one final piece to consider. Do you like them? If the answer is no, I would get the hell out of there. If your gut is uneasy, move along. He/She is not the right one for you.

"While fee-only is a far better way to deliver service and advice, it doesn't guarantee competence or even honesty. Investors must still do their due diligence when selecting an advisor."

- **Frank Armstrong III**, *The Informed Investor*

85

THE FEE-ONLY PLANNER

This type of financial advisor can make a world of difference for the average person. What is the difference between them and the fee-only advisor? In the simplest of explanations, an advisor might help you with your investments only. A planner would help you with all of your money matters, which would include planning for retirement, insurance, taxes, debt payment plans, Social Security strategies, and much more.

The fee-only planner provides insight into many parts of your financial situation far beyond your investments. There is real value there if you can find the right person or team to help you. Let's take a step back, first. Do you need a fee-only person just for investments? If so, look for an investment advisor that is fee-only. If you want more from your advisor, look for a certified financial planner (CFP) that will assist you with many issues beyond basic asset allocation.

If you need a fee-only planner, I would strongly recommend starting with napfa.org. There are many qualified people who could work with you in putting together a financial plan that deals with today and long into the future. This organization focuses on the importance of working for the client above all else. Saying that, you should be very selective with whom you select. Like any field, there are poor certified financial planners.

Do I use one? No, but I love this stuff and I am always reading up on this subject AND I stay up on the issues when things change, and they are always changing. Is that you? If it is, you may join me in going it alone. Here is where you have to be brutally honest with yourself. Are you going to commit to helping yourself? That means educating yourself on the matter and then acting on that education.

Many people won't do it, or they just can't for one reason or another. This makes the case for the fee-only planner IF you have the minimum amount of funds to access their help. It usually runs between $100,000 - $500,000. You don't have that much? Contact your local NAPFA financial advisor for guidance. They might be able to get you in contact with someone who works by the project or the hour (the Garrett Financial Planners would be an option here). Spending a few hundred dollars for these temporary services could be worth it.

What questions do you ask when selecting a planner? I would stick with the questions you just reviewed in the previous chapter. They will serve you well with your search. Do not underestimate the value of a human being sitting down with you and covering all of these matters in detail. You might consider them as your financial conscience. They keep you focused when life gets busy or scary.

A good fee-only planner will provide that human touch that many people desire. That is hard to achieve if your advisor or planner works over the Internet, phone, or message board. Do not underestimate this point when selecting a planner. If you don't like them, find one you do. Don't settle for a rotten human being just because he or she is good at asset allocation and other money matters. They should be worthy of becoming your friend. If not, move on.

The fee-only industry is gradually picking up steam as more and more people become educated on these matters. Take your time and evaluate these people very carefully before selecting someone to help you. It could be a relationship that lasts for many decades. Make it a good one!

"The only thing I'm absolutely 100% sure of is that the lower the fee I pay to the purveyor of the investment service, the more there is going to be for me. And that's why index funds work."

- **Burton Malkiel**, Author of *A Random Walk Down Wall Street*

86

THE INSTITUTIONAL INVESTOR

The institutional investor consists of large organizations that pool large sums of money. Here I am talking about pension funds that are managed by corporations and state governments. This would also include insurance companies and banks. This also pertains to large endowments like Yale and Harvard. Finally, this also includes many large non-profit organizations that end up managing millions if not billions of dollars. Many individuals are indirectly investing through these organizations.

Collectively, they have done a poor job in the past when investing the money entrusted to them. Poor job? They have failed to capture the market returns. Why? Wall Street comes a-knocking every time requests are made by those large organizations to manage these large pots of money. There is a great deal of money at stake and Wall Street wants their cut! How much? In many cases, you are looking at .5% or more.

That's not much, right? When you combine that with their inability to capture market return (add another .5% or so), you end up with institutional investors failing collectively, by about 1% per year. Let's say you have a State Pension Plan with $28 billion dollars in the fund. **If you subtract 1% from that $28 billion, you get $280 million!** Per year, that money is lost to fees, commissions, loads, and underperformance. That percentage could be closer to 2% in many cases!

That is happening all over America today. Are you connected to one of these organizations? Do you have a loved one who is? How much is in that fund that you are counting on? Go ahead and look it up; it's all public knowledge. Once you find that big number, take 1% of it and see just how much is being lost to Wall Street.

What can be done? The answer can be found on your doorstep. Stop looking at politicians and Wall Street to fix the problem. YOU fix the problem. You and I have to raise hell to the people who run these large funds throughout America and force change. Start digging into the details to see how much is being spent per year as they reach for returns beyond the market returns. It will shock you in many cases.

I am currently struggling with the State of Iowa over their pension system, IPERS. It's a mess and it is actually doing better than the majority of other pension funds. Don't be in a hurry to pat them on the back, though. They are getting a D on their report card when others are getting an F! This large state pension is forking out well over $100 million per year in costs alone. **Their costs could be lower than $15 million per year**.

Hundreds of millions of dollars have gone to Wall Street and its many "helpers" instead of the people who need it the most. Here I am talking about the pensioners who worked for decades as teachers, firefighters, policeman, etc....

When will things change? When we, collectively, say we have had enough of this system that feeds Wall Street at the expense of pensioners and taxpayers. When we become educated well enough to understand the matter and demand the change that is needed within these organizations, change can start to take place.

You can look no further than the Thrift Savings Plan (tsp.gov) for an example of how an institutional plan could be run at minimal cost. The total yearly fees are around .03% per year. It's time for a change!

"Any pension fund manager who doesn't have the vast majority—and I mean 70% or 80% of his or her portfolio—in passive investments is guilty of malfeasance, nonfeasance or some other kind of bad feasance!"

- **Merton Miller**, Nobel Laureate in Economics

87

THE FUTURE

I am going to do something I tell you not to do. I am going to predict the future! Well, not so much predict the future as much as tell you what I want the future to look like for the average investor. The future could be a lovely place when enough people reach a high enough level of financial education. Let's take a look at this "new world."

The fee-based advisor goes away. With time, the average person becomes educated on this fee-based business model that serves everyone well except the actual investor. Fee-only financial advisors replace the fee-based advisors throughout countries all over the world.

The fee-only advisors compete for the business of the informed investor. Yearly fees drop as more investors demand low costs in their portfolio. All index portfolios become standard practice for individual and institutional investors as more and more people are exposed to the research demonstrating probabilities that outweigh possibilities.

The number of fee-only advisors expands dramatically as more advisors see and feel the real benefit of helping people rather than fleecing them. Basically, the heart and soul is brought back to the financial services industry. The investor wins, the advisor wins, and society wins.

The fee-only world separates into fee-only advisors that focus on strategic asset allocation using index funds and fee-only planners who assist people with many issues beyond just investing. The investor who wants help selects an advisor or planner based on their specific needs. There will be room for them all as the fee-based advisors exit the scene.

When will this happen? As soon as enough people like you and me become educated on the matter. That's the solution. When we collectively become educated on how this game is played, we will force change by rejecting the poor choices marketed to us today.

Will government fix this problem? No, they can't. You can take all of their hollow promises (republicans and democrats) and toss them aside. Politicians, more times than not, run in after change has happened. They will come in at the end and take credit for what you and I did.

What about Wall Street? Will they fix themselves? I laugh as I write that last rhetorical question. Wall Street will not voluntarily reduce their paychecks and stop their business model when it works so well for them. It is ridiculous to think otherwise. They will change when they are forced to change and no sooner. Informed investors force change.

The financial industry and their many "helpers" will change when the individual and institutional investors demand it. Slowly, but surely, that is happening as more and more people move toward all index portfolios that are passively managed at the lowest possible costs. As our ranks become larger, the market place will move in some very big ways.

What about the life insurance industry? The informed investor will see through the marketing campaigns that guarantee you mediocre returns as they lock up your money over long periods of time. They will stop investing in life insurance products. Welcome to the future!

"Put 10% of the cash in short-term government bonds and 90% in a very low-cost S&P 500 index fund. (I suggest Vanguard's.) I believe the trust's long-term results from this policy will be superior to those attained by most investors — whether pension funds, institutions or individuals — who employ high-fee managers."

- **Warren Buffett**, Advice given to the trustee when he passes

88

HOW TO DO IT

I know some of you have jumped right to this chapter. That was a mistake. Please go back and read the previous chapters before reading this one. For those of you who have read each chapter, here goes.

- Get rid of high interest rate debt as fast as possible before investing.

- Save at least 10% of your gross income and strive to make it 20%.

- Decide how much you want to own in stocks vs. bonds/cash.

- Divide your money up using stock and bond index mutual funds.

- Invest in retirement accounts whenever possible.

- Keep your expenses below .3% and try to get them below .1%.

- Automatically invest into those accounts every month.

- Strongly consider investing in international markets.

- Consider a REIT index fund to capture the total economy.

- Consider small and value stock index funds as your portfolio grows.

- Buy and hold. Rebalance when the allocations get out of whack.

- Stay the course and seek out a fee-only advisor when you need help.

Those specifics are all you need to know to make you one of the best investors in the world. I promise you that, but you have to defend yourself against all of the obstacles that move you away from them. That is why the previous chapters of the book were so important. Small things can actually hide really big things.

Think of an iceberg. What you see sticking out of the water is miniscule compared to what is under the water. Those details that are covered in this chapter are what is sticking out of the water. Your knowledge is what lies below the surface. It is incredibly important to gather the knowledge prior to making investment decisions.

How do you know if you are ready to apply what you have learned? You read each one of those bullets and you clearly understand them AND you understand what goes into making them. You grasp the many nuances that formulate those ideas. You have taken the complicated and made it simple with your financial education.

As you continue to increase your investing knowledge, you are sure to have that "aha" moment. Aha? The "aha" moment is that instant in time when it all comes together in your head. You get it. It all makes sense to you now and you understand how you can apply it to your life. You can sit down and explain it to others as well. You have transformed into a new person. You have become the wise and successful investor.

Congratulations!

"Steer a careful course in a balanced investment program; seek the lowest costs; rely on highly diversified bond and stock index funds; demand tax efficiency; trade infrequently; be skeptical that past market returns and the performance of hot fund managers will repeat; and keep a long-term perspective. Then, stay the course."

- **John Bogle**, *Common Sense on Mutual Funds*

89

COMING FULL CIRCLE

Once you become the wise and successful investor, it's your turn to help others. You deserve credit for what you have completed and certainly a pat on the back, but you're not done. It's time to turn back and provide a helping hand to others who need assistance and guidance. Here is a little secret. I have benefited much more in my life from helping others change their lives than when I actually did it for myself. Let's take a look.

At age 25, I set forth on my journey of financial enlightenment. What I learned very early in the process was how much I did not know and what I did know was mostly wrong. I felt empty. I felt dumb. I felt as if I had wasted a lot of time and energy. You could say I took a punch from the financial services industry. It hurt and it knocked me on my butt. I got up.

I associate this to being hit by a bully. I took their best punch and it almost knocked me out, but I got up and stood up to those bullies dressed in suits. They backed down!

I found out that bully wasn't so tough after all. He was more show than brawn. I pushed him and his expensive products aside and moved on with my life. That's when I started experiencing big changes that would forever change the course of my life. I was empowered and no bully was going to stop me again.

It wasn't always easy. I had plenty of support from the authors in the books I was reading, but not so much from the people who surrounded me in everyday life. I had to stay a bit stubborn as I took that leap of faith in what I was learning from "my team" that was found in those books. I'm glad I did. I decided to believe in ME.

This brings me back to helping others. By showing others the path, encouraging them along the way, and giving them a nudge when necessary to stay on that path, I get to experience the human "transformation" that I experienced again and again with others.

Transformation? It's something I learned from a guy by the name of Joseph Campbell. He taught me that we could change into our new selves only when we let our old selves die. This metaphorical death helps us transform into something better.

It's a wonderful thing to behold when you see someone take control of their finances AND their life. Taking control of your money can be life altering. I have seen people change in ways that are not easy to explain. I can usually see it before they see it. At some point the person you are helping "transforms." Trust me, this is real.

We can take it one step further by turning back and helping others. As Joseph Campbell would say, we come full circle. He calls it the hero's journey and it's a journey worth taking as we reach back to show others the path leading to financial freedom. This path takes you down a corridor of not only financial freedom, but also a path toward finding meaning in life. You end up finding YOU along the way.

It's a powerful thing when you apply this process of learning, and then changing, and then circling back to help others do the same. It might surprise you just how good it will make you feel to see someone change with the help you provide them. Reach out and share what you have learned. Be ready and willing to help your fellow human being. Lives will change and you will have completed the hero's journey.

"When we quit thinking primarily about ourselves and our own self-preservation, we undergo a truly heroic transformation of consciousness."

- **Joseph Campbell**

90

THIS IS IT

I have taken you as far as I can. It's time to hand over the keys so you can take control of your investing life. I have provided you with many of the answers you will need to not only become a great investor, but hopefully, a person who shares that knowledge with others. You see, this book is about a lot more than just investing. It's about life.

It's about challenging the world in which we live. It's about knocking down barriers that reside not only outside of us, but inside of us. This is about transforming into a new person as you set out to create your new life. It's about creating your future.

To become the wise and successful investor you must avoid the crooks, the "helpers," the expensive products, and all of the mistakes that come with those obstacles. It doesn't occur overnight. Little by little, you must accumulate the information, apply it to your life, be patient with the results, and then reap the rewards. Complete the process by sharing what you know with others. That will be your ultimate reward.

I would like to share a true story that I shared in my book, *Financial Happine$$*. This story explains the value of this message I am sharing with you and I hope it provides some answers on why you should take this journey toward becoming the wise and successful investor.

Once upon a time, there was a young man who came home for the holidays. He showed up with something other than presents. He came with knowledge, financial knowledge to be precise. As his father was sitting down with his favorite beverage, this young man sat beside him and started to share what he had learned.

The young man started to talk about this *new world* and how it had changed his life. He explained how it had empowered him and how he had been exposed to something new that he didn't know existed. His father listened carefully, but he needed some convincing.

What could a young man without a college education teach this older man who had lived a long and rather difficult life? *Plenty* was the response from his enthusiastic and highly animated son. And at that, the young man showed his father the portfolio of assets he had accumulated. His father came to realize that his son had more money than he did. Maybe it was time to listen.

I was that young man. My financial education gave me the ability to help not only myself but also my father. We moved his life savings away from a broker who was churning his account (buying and selling securities often to increase the amount of commissions paid to the broker) and into a no-load index mutual fund that would not.

My life changed when I came to the realization that it was up to me to change it. No one was going to fly in and rescue me. Once I accepted that thought, my life improved in some pretty big ways. I took control of my life. Financial freedom followed!

You can do this. Believe in yourself. Believe that you have everything you need within you to change the course of your life and the lives of others. Challenge what you see as you ask not only yourself, but others, the question I posed to you at the beginning of this book:

What Color is the Sky?

"The world is his, who can see through its pretension… See it to be a lie, and you have already dealt it its mortal blow."

- **Ralph Waldo Emerson**

Acknowledgments

Many people have helped me. I needed their guidance, their editing abilities, and maybe most of all, I needed their support. I am very grateful to the people who helped make this happen. There are simply too many names to put down on paper, but you know who you are. Thank you from the bottom of my heart.

A book is not written in a few weeks or even in a few months (at least not by me). A book is written using a lifetime of experience and knowledge. When I think back to my family, friends, coaches, and teachers (in and outside the classroom), I am struck by how many wonderful people have entered my life and provided me insight when I needed it most.

I needed assistance, and many of you were there to provide your help and support when I needed it most. Thank you for your help and that occasional kick in the butt that I needed. We build our life based on our experiences with others.

I also want to thank people I have never met. Those authors who write books that change our lives are saviors to many of us. They expand our world far beyond anything we could have imagined. They show us what we can become and where we can go.

Those independent sources enlighten us and maybe most importantly, they provide hope as we try to figure out where we fit in this crazy world. Thank you for taking the time and making the effort to teach a young kid from a small town in Iowa that he could be anything he wanted to be if he was willing to put in the time and effort. You changed my life, and I truly appreciate what you have done to make this world a better place.

Illustrations

The illustrations in the book, including the book cover, were designed and created by some very talented ladies.

Book cover creator: Meghan Kelley
Book cover design: Faith Wittrock
Stage I illustration: Melanie Walde

Appendix A

Recommended Reading:

Burton Malkiel

A Random Walk Down Wall Street (A classic that provides insight into a world that can be mysterious to us all.)

John Bogle

The Little Book of Common Sense Investing (This is a great starter book on investing. You can trust John Bogle. I do.)

Common Sense on Mutual Funds (Mr. Bogle will teach you all you need and want to know about investing in mutual funds.)

William Bernstein

The Intelligent Asset-Allocator (William Bernstein can definitely help you better understand the subject of asset allocation.)

The Four Pillars of Investing (The finest book on investing I have ever read. This book will show you the past, the present and maybe the future.)

The Investors Manifesto (A great follow-up book. You might find this an easier read than his other books.)

Charles Ellis

Winning the Loser's Game (Investing becomes easier with knowledge.)

Frank Armstrong III

The Informed Investor (Easy to read and he gets right to the point.)

Daniel Solin

The Smartest Investment Book You'll Ever Read (This is short and easy.)

The Smartest Retirement Book You'll Ever Read (Short and easy, Part II.)

Jason Zweig

Your Money & Your Brain (Explains how your brain works against you!)

Rick Ferri

The Power of Passive Investing (Rick lays out the facts for all to see.)

All About Asset Allocation (Rick provides the blueprint in a simple way.)

Mark T. Hebner

Index Funds: The 12-Step Recovery Program for Active Investors (This book lays it all out. A must read and a pretty easy one.)

Andrew Hallam

Millionaire Teacher: The Nine Rules of Wealth You Should Have learned in School (The average guy can do it. Andrew Hallam is your example.)

Burton Malkiel and Charles Ellis

The Elements of Investing (Short and to the point. A very easy read.)

Larry Swedroe

Chasing Alpha (Cuts through the crap and provides the facts.)

The Only Guide to Alternative Investments You'll Ever Need (Insightful!)

Glossary

1035 exchange: A transfer of money from one insurance policy (this includes annuities) to another. This type of exchange can be used when moving money out of high-fee insurance policies and into low-fee insurance policies. Educate yourself carefully regarding any possible surrender charges.

401(k): A defined contribution plan offered by a corporation to its employees to set aside tax-deferred income for retirement purposes. This is the place where you can grow your money tax-deferred (traditional version) or tax-free (Roth version).

403(b): A retirement plan offered by nonprofit organizations, such as universities and charitable organizations, rather than corporations. This is simply a company retirement plan that goes by a different name. Fees tend to be high compared to other defined contribution plans.

457(b): A retirement plan offered by some nonprofits, as well as state and local governments. This is another company retirement plan that goes by a different name. One big plus with this type of plan is the elimination of the 10% penalty for early withdrawal. This means you can take out money prior to age 59.5 without penalties.

529 Plan: An education savings plan designed to help parents save for their children's college education. Go straight to the state and bypass the broker. Shop around. Some states have poor choices and others provide very good options that include index funds from Vanguard.

Active management: The attempt to uncover securities (stocks and bonds, for example) that the market has misidentified as being under or overvalued. This involves outsmarting and outmaneuvering the other smart people in the room. The past has shown us it doesn't work with any degree of consistency (pure chance basically). Avoid the people who tell you they can provide it. They can't.

Annuity: An investment that is a contract backed by an insurance company. Its main benefit is that it allows your money to compound and grow without taxation until withdrawal. The main drawbacks include high commissions, high fees, and difficulty in extracting your money. The financial industry loves annuities. That is a good reason to question the benefit of an annuity to you. Stay away, far away.

Asset allocation: The process of dividing up one's securities among broad asset classes (stocks, bonds, and real estate, for example). This may include domestic and foreign stocks and bonds. The asset allocation should be identified only after the investor identifies their risk tolerance, time horizon, and specific goals that are unique to their particular situation.

Asset class: A group of assets with similar risk and expected return characteristics. Cash, debt instruments (think bonds), real estate (REITS or rental real estate), and equities (stocks) are a few examples. There are more specific classes that are broken down within an asset class, such as large and small company stocks and domestic and international stocks.

Benchmark: A standard against which mutual funds and other investment vehicles can be judged. Small-cap managers should be judged against a small-cap index such as the Russell 2000 Index. Large-cap growth funds should be judged against a large-cap growth index such as the S&P 500 Index. Comparing apples to apples is the point of using the proper benchmark.

Bond: A loan that investors make to a corporation or government. The investor provides the capital, and the other party promises a specified return. Bonds generally pay a set amount of interest on a regular basis. All bonds have a maturity date when the bond issuer must pay back the bond at full value to the bondholders (the lenders).

Broker: A person who acts as an intermediary for the purchase or sale of investments. Almost all brokers are paid on commission, which creates a conflict of interest with their clients (also known as victims). The more the broker sells the more money he makes. This is called churning, and it is illegal but difficult to prove in a court of law. Stay away from them.

Capital gain: The profit from selling your stock at a higher price than the price for which it was purchased. Example: You bought a mutual fund at $60 per share, and you sell it five years later for $90 per share. Your profit is $30 per share. If your investment is outside of a retirement account, you will pay a capital gains tax on that profit. This will not apply (in the year in which you sold the asset) to an investment that is in a retirement plan.

Cash-value life insurance: This is the type of life insurance that most life insurance agents recommend. In a cash-value policy, you buy life insurance coverage but also get a savings account to boot. The investment returns tend to be poor because of the high commissions and high fees that come out in the early years of the policy. Stay away.

Churning: When a broker has you buying and selling your investments often to feed HIS bank account. It is illegal, but practiced often as the broker rationalizes the extensive trading. A broker needs a lot of activity on your account otherwise the commissions will not be enough to feed his lifestyle. Avoid brokers, and you will avoid being churned. It doesn't get any simpler than that.

Data mining: Many "helpers" and organizations in the industry go back and retrieve data and then use it to convince the uninformed investor about the future based on that past data that was selected to make their argument. Be on guard for this and see through its lies. This deceitful approach leaves out a great deal of information they would prefer you not to know about.

Defined benefit plan: A pension that your employer promises you based on time with the company, your earnings, and usually your age. These are going away and being replaced with defined contribution plans. These types of plans are still widely available for state and federal employees. If you have one, count your blessings.

Defined contribution plan: A retirement plan funded primarily by the employee. It may come in the form of a traditional or a Roth version. Names of these types of plans are as follows: 401(k), 403(b), 457(b), and TSP (thrift savings plan). You must feed these accounts monthly and yearly if you want a comfortable retirement.

Diversification: Dividing investment funds among a variety of investments with different risk/return characteristics to minimize portfolio risk. A mutual fund that owns 3,000 companies is one example.

Dividend: The income paid to investors holding an investment. The dividend is a portion of a company's profits paid to its shareholders. For assets held outside retirement accounts, dividends are taxable in most cases.

Dollar-cost averaging: A fixed amount of money is invested regularly and periodically. When the price of the asset is down, more shares are purchased. When the price of the asset is up, fewer shares are purchased.

Equity: Equity is a term often used to describe stocks. In real estate, it is used to describe the difference between how much your home is worth and how much you owe. Example: Your home is worth $200,000 and you owe $120,000. Your equity is $80,000.

Exchange traded funds (ETFs): Like mutual funds, they can be created to represent virtually any index or asset class. Like stocks (but unlike mutual funds), they trade on a stock exchange throughout the day. They work for long-term, lump-sum investing. They don't work for investors who trade often and/or dollar-cost average money into their investments.

Expense ratio: The operating expenses of a mutual fund expressed as a percentage of total assets. They cover manager fees, administrative costs, and sometimes marketing costs.

Fee-based financial advisor/planner: This term is used to describe how a licensed salesperson earns his or her money. Fee-based usually means the salesperson works on commissions from the investments he or she sells and some other method such as a percentage of money under management or an hourly fee. Avoid fee-based salespeople.

Fee-only financial advisor/planner: This term describes how a professional earns his or her money. The drawback with this type of planner is they generally require a large amount of money under management before they work with you.

Fiduciary: The expert sitting across from you has an obligation to act in your best interest instead of his. When seeking financial advice, this is the kind of person you should seek. Sadly, they are hard to find.

Fixed annuity: An insurance contract in which fixed dollar payments are paid for the term of the contract. The insurance company guarantees both earnings and principal. A high initial teaser rate is generally offered to pull you in. High commissions, high fees, and high surrender costs make this a poor option.

Index mutual fund: A mutual fund designed to mimic the returns of a given market. Examples would include: S&P 500, Wilshire 5000, and the Russell 3000. These types of funds are ultra-cheap, and because of the cost difference, they have consistently beaten managed mutual funds over short and long periods of time. Never pay a load when selecting this option.

Individual retirement account (IRA): A retirement account that you open outside of your place of employment. There are many types: Roth (after tax) and traditional (before tax) are two. Which one you select will vary based on your current and projected tax situation. There are many rules as well as contribution limits to these accounts.

Institutional investors: Large investment organizations, including insurance companies, depositary institutions, pension funds, and philanthropies. Indirectly, your money is invested through them when you have a pension, give to a charity, etc.

International stock market mutual fund: Pooled stocks within a mutual fund that are invested in stock markets outside of the United States. This may include developed countries like Germany, Canada, France, and Japan or developing countries like Brazil, India, China, and Russia. The latter is identified as emerging markets.

Investment Management Company: A company whose main business is holding securities of other companies for purely investment purposes. The investment company invests money on behalf of its shareholders, who in turn share in the profits and losses.

Junk bond: A bond rated below investment grade. These types of bonds are also called high-yield bonds. Many people own junk bonds as they chase yield (interest on your investment). You do not need junk and that includes high-yield mutual funds.

Keogh plan: A tax-deductible retirement plan that is available to self-employed individuals. They are relatively easy to set up at your favorite investment management company, such as Vanguard.

Large-cap: Large-cap stocks are those companies considered big relative to other companies, as measured by their market capitalization. Large can be subjective.

Load mutual fund: A mutual fund sold with a sales charge and paid to the salesperson that initiates the action between the investor and the investment company. A load and a commission are one in the same.

Mutual fund: A portfolio of stocks, bonds, or other assets managed by an investment company. They provide wide diversification that is necessary and prudent for the average investor.

No-load mutual fund: A mutual fund sold without a sales or distribution fee. There is no commission attached to your investment.

Nominal return: Returns that have not been adjusted for inflation. These are the types of returns you will almost always see when reading a newspaper, a magazine, or listening to a presentation on investing.

Passive management: A buy-and-hold investment strategy. The passive management approach includes lower portfolio turnover, lower operating expenses and transactions costs, greater tax efficiency, consistent exposure to risk factors over time, and a long-term perspective.

Real estate investment trust (REIT): A mutual fund that owns stock in shopping centers, apartment buildings, and other commercial real estate. Focus on owning publicly traded REITs while staying away from Private REITs pushed hard by commission-hungry brokers.

Real return: The nominal return minus the inflation rate. Example: You earn 5 percent on an investment and the inflation rate is running at 3.2 percent. Your real return would be 1.8 percent.

Rebalancing: The process of buying and selling portfolio components so as to maintain a target asset allocation.

Recency bias: An investor is overly influenced by recent events when selecting a particular asset.

Roth: A retirement plan that places your money into your selected investment accounts after the money has been taxed.

Russell 1000 index: This index is intended to track 1,000 of the largest publicly traded companies in America. It is used as a benchmark for large-capitalization stocks.

Russell 2000 index: This index is intended to track 2,000 of the smallest publicly traded companies in America. This index is used as a benchmark of small-capitalization stocks.

Russell 3000 index: This index tracks the Russell 1000 and 2000 index of companies. It is used to replicate the entire market of large and small companies.

Simplified employee pension individual retirement account (SEP-IRA): A retirement plan for self-employed people.

Standard & Poor's 500 Index: An index that measures the performance of 500 large-company US stocks.

Stock: Shares of ownership in a publicly held company. You can invest in stock by purchasing individual shares or by owning a stock mutual fund.

Survivorship bias: Mutual funds that die don't count against the overall return as if they never existed. Managed mutual fund historical returns would look much worse if all of the headstones were counted.

Target date retirement fund: This type of fund allocates your investments within the fund based on the date you select. A 2050 fund will be more aggressive (more stocks) than a 2030 fund (more bonds and cash).

Term life insurance: Inexpensive life insurance that has no cash value. It should be purchased when someone relies on your income to live.

Thrift Savings Plan (TSP): A defined contribution plan offered by the federal government to its employees (military and civilian).

Timeshare: You are renting a really nice place for a week or so during the year. They call it buying. Avoid them and the salespeople who push them. They are expensive to maintain and difficult to sell. Don't fall for the pitch.

Turnover: The portion of a portfolio that is traded in a given period of time. For example, a portfolio with an annual turnover of 300 percent will increase the costs by approximately 3 percent per year.

Universal life insurance: Cash-value life insurance that grew out of whole life insurance. Part investment and part insurance is the idea. Stay away.

Variable annuity: A life insurance contract providing future payments to the holder. The size of the future payments will depend on the performance of the portfolio's securities, as well as the investor's age at the time of annuitization and prevailing interest rates. Stay away.

Variable life insurance: A cash-value policy that has part of the account invested in investments like stocks and bonds that will fluctuate over time. Stay away. The costs are high and the returns are low.

Whole life insurance: Cash-value life insurance that provides level premiums over time. High commissions and high fees make this a bad deal.

Wilshire 5000 total market index: This index mimics the entire US stock market, which includes small, mid, and large capitalization companies. Use this index when identifying a total stock market fund to invest in.

Made in the USA
Monee, IL
04 May 2021

67711065R10132